GALLOP

GALLOP

SUE LYON-HEAP

ILLUSTRATIONS BY SUE LYON-HEAP

Matador
9 Priory Business Park,
Wistow Road, Kibworth Beauchamp,
Leicestershire. LE8 0RX
Tel: 0116 279 2299
Email: books@troubador.co.uk
Web: www.troubador.co.uk/matador
Twitter: @matadorbooks

ISBN 978 1788034 593

British Library Cataloguing in Publication Data.
A catalogue record for this book is available from the British Library.

Printed and bound by CPI Group (UK) Ltd, Croydon, CR0 4YY
Typeset in 11pt Minion Pro by Troubador Publishing Ltd, Leicester, UK

Matador is an imprint of Troubador Publishing Ltd

This story is for Simon, Emma, Freddie and Jack, whose own exploits and aspirations give me no end of fun, interest and pleasure.

CONTENTS

INTRODUCTION

Horses are 95 percent disappointment, but the other 5 percent makes up for it.

I wonder who said those words. They ring with such truth, and I did hear they may have been said by the late Queen Elizabeth the Queen Mother.

It was the day of the Grand National in 1956, and the air was buzzing with expectation amongst racing and sporting enthusiasts. The reason was a particular horse. His name was Devon Loch, his jockey was Dick Francis, and his owner was the Queen Mother. She had never won the race, but this time her horse would have thousands on the edge of their seats – Devon Loch was strongly fancied to win.

Chattering, eager crowds surged towards the famous racecourse at Aintree on the outskirts of the city of Liverpool. Hundreds more crammed into pubs in all corners of the land, and especially in Liverpool, where in a haze of tobacco smoke, and pints on a table, men with a bob or two on the big race listened, with heads together, huddled round a crackly wireless set. It was a different world in those days, and television – black and white – was still a novel experience; unbelievably the Grand National was not televised until four years later, in 1960. Austerity remained evident as a grey Britain rebuilt and recovered from the bombing and scrimping of WW2, while children from the cities continued to play on heaps of rubble. Food rationing had ceased just two years earlier. The only way to view the race, apart from being there, was on the Pathé News – also black and white – at the cinema.

You could say that my father, Reginald, enjoyed a drink rather more than was good for him, and he also enjoyed National Hunt racing – and a punt. On that Grand National day, March 24th 1956, he had a rosy twinkle in his eye, as he had put money on the Queen Mother's horse – and to a greater degree than usual. He was in buoyant mood, and my mother, Grace, was out for the afternoon, sitting round a bridge table studying the cards in her hand – probably with her good friend, Peggy Sangster, mother of Robert, who was one of the noted triumvirate, with Irish trainer Vincent O'Brien and John Magnier, who would became the most famous racehorse owners of their time. Set up for the afternoon, Reggie had his customary tipple to hand – gin and vermouth and a cube of ice dropped with a clunk into the sizeable glass, with the ready top-up nearby, while next to this rested his pipe in a large crystal ashtray along with the familiar squashy pouch of tobacco.

My father was slightly built and not very tall but he was a dapper figure, and on that day he sported a natty dark green bow tie with bright white spots. Sitting comfortably, legs crossed in a winged armchair, he listened intently to the BBC commentary as the excitement built up at Aintree. As the big race gained momentum he was quickly on his feet. Head cocked as he leant closer to the radio, known as a wireless, he picked up the distinctive voice of a young – and one day to become the outstanding racing commentator of all racing commentators – Peter O'Sullevan, who was apparently standing on the bonnet of a white van for a better view (remember this was 1956) and calling the race at the 14th fence, the 28th on the second circuit, and two fences from home.

The distinctive gold tassel adorning the black cap of the Queen Mother's horse was in a prominent position, and gaining ground as the horses streamed towards the end of the course. They leapt the final fence, and Devon Loch stuck his head out and powered ahead. Now the hats were coming off – up in the air they flew, and the heaving stands rocked. Sensing victory Reggie beamed with delight, took another quick sip, and raised his arm in triumph, eyes shining. This was going to be a National win for Her Majesty – and for himself. Then – silence, and the great cheering stopped – just for a split second. Through the hush came the crushing voice of the commentator, and my father's arm fell to his side.

'He's down, Devon Loch is down.'

It is an achingly long way from the last fence to the winning post at Aintree, nearly 500 yards. After four miles and thirty fences, horses are leg-weary and many lose heart. The cacophony of sound along that final stretch had risen to a mighty roar as Devon Loch galloped valiantly on, when, with no warning, the horse appeared to belly flop onto the track, all four legs splayed out, his head up and looking ahead, seemingly with his eye on the winning post. He was up again in seconds, regained his feet, and walked away unharmed. By his side, head down, shoulders hunched, and gutted, was his jockey, Dick Francis. But it was gone – in a flash the moment of impending, glorious victory had been whipped away from horse, jockey and owner. ESB, ridden by Dave Dick, galloped on to win.

There was never any concrete explanation for what happened, and despite his illustrious career Dick Francis never did win the Grand National, and neither did the Queen Mother. Even now I feel a sense of sadness for my father as I recall the dejection on his face.

I have thought about the opening words of this story many times, and the typically stoic sentiments, perhaps, from a lady who had championed National Hunt racing for decades.

If they touch your life horses can bring incomparable elation, but also trauma. Years later those words returned to me. The date was Friday

9th December 2011, but it was not disappointment I experienced that day; it was fear – cold, numb fear, that gripped like a vice.

A pristine nurse had quietly ushered me into a small side room off the Intensive Care Unit at Frenchay Hospital, Bristol. In the hushed ward, on the other side of the door, lay my daughter, Polly, in a coma with head injuries as a result of a fall from a horse. She had been like that since about 5pm the day before. We had had ponies and horses for over fifty years. I was used to news of horse falls – cuts, bruises, and a few broken collar bones – but I knew as soon as I got the call that this was different. It was Polly's sister, Tory, who had rung us at home in Cheshire at around 8pm the evening before. She came quickly to the point.

'Polly has had a fall. She has a serious head injury. She is unconscious, and on life support at Frenchay Hospital. It does not look good.'

We had raced down an empty motorway through the night, my husband Geoffrey and I, with two Jack Russell terriers curled up on the back seat, a canary swaying in a cage, and a few clothes thrown into a suitcase. Urgently, we left behind an aged horse in the paddock with a feed and a net of hay, and a frantically locked up house. Halfway down the motorway the mobile buzzed, and I snatched it up. Pressing the phone to my ear, a far off voice came through the engine drone of the car.

'They want to insert probes into Polly's head.' It was Polly's husband, Toby. 'There is an element of risk but necessary.'

I drew a tiny twinge of reassurance that things were happening. Polly was fighting, still hanging on. The motorway stretched long and bleak. Geoffrey kept his foot down, the dogs slept on, and the little yellow canary clung to his perch, a bit of brightness in that grim car. It was now the following morning. I watched the closed door, and waited for the consultant to give his verdict. With me were Toby, and Geoffrey, Polly's stepfather. None of us spoke, but the tension quivered all around in that small room. The door opened, the consultant came in, then someone closed the door quietly behind him.

Polly is well known and respected in the world of three day eventing. She has competed at Badminton and Burghley, and as a former British International, the winner of six European team and individual gold medals during her Junior and Young Rider days. Some of her team mates in those early years would become household names within the sport. Among them were William Fox-Pitt, Pippa Funnell and Tina Cook.

On that wintry afternoon in December at her training base, Charlton Park, Malmesbury, Wiltshire, Polly was having a normal day. She had competed all morning at an indoor competition, and in the afternoon she mounted a smart horse belonging to a client and trotted off to the all-weather school for some training. As a chilly dusk fell and the business of evening stables began, with horses whickering for a feed, stable beds turned over for the night, rugs adjusted and water buckets filled, she would set off home to her two small sons, Freddie, aged six and Jack, aged two. But that never happened. A breeze blew into a raging gale; branches tossed and the wind moaned through rustling trees. The smart horse Polly was riding wheeled round, stood up on his hind legs, lost his balance, and crashed to the ground. Half a ton of solid animal squashed her into oblivion.

The consultant looked at the three of us. 'With this type of head injury one third of patients may die, but Polly has age on her side, and she is supremely fit.'

That's a glimmer of hope, I thought, eyeing him as he spoke, making sure I missed nothing. He continued, 'The next twenty-four to forty-eight hours are critical. To prevent further damage to the brain, we must stabilise Polly, and she will be kept in an induced coma.'

I knew my daughter's make-up, from cracked ribs, while competing on horses, to the bloody-minded and fighting spirit that was her nature. Deeply unconscious she might be, but if ever there was a time she needed those particular characteristics, it was now.

I had heard about people who kept long vigils bending over a hospital bed, looking, listening, and desperate for a sign that there was life there. The clawing dread of being told that the life support machines should be switched off, and the thoughts that rushed through my head; *What will happen to Freddie and Jack, my two little grandsons?* And which were quickly pushed away. But we had come through the first night, the black pit of nightmare. Polly was alive, that meant hope, and from that chink of light I forced myself to believe that she would eventually wake up.

The expression a stiff upper lip seems to be out of fashion for the more liberal-minded today, but my parents were of that generation and upbringing, and my mother Grace viewed adversity as a challenge to be overcome. A powerful and charismatic personality, with elegant looks to match, she had a zest for life, possessed a distinct hauteur, and was quick-witted and courageous. During those long days at Frenchay Hospital, I had to repeat to myself her frequent sayings.

'Don't give up. We don't go under. Put your best foot forward. Don't foist your problems onto other people. Smile – you look more attractive!'

I was in for a long haul of horrible uncertainty. How could I fend off the fears, and turn this crashing episode into some kind of positive, however small? Polly was still, eyes shut, and in every bed someone lay critically ill and unconscious; but in that sombre ward there was quiet activity. There were nurses, doctors, a few visitors – just the close relatives. I realised that other people would go through this experience. I was not alone. I had a thought, and searching in my bag for a pen and any scrap of paper, I began to write a journal about what was happening around me, and especially to Polly. As the hours stretched to days, and weeks, those scribbles helped to channel my emotions positively. Hospital units were not unfamiliar territory. I had followed the blue light on more than one occasion. I will briefly return to my journal in Frenchay Hospital, and Polly's battle for recovery, but this is not a story about Polly's accident, as she has covered that in her own highly readable book, *Where did I go?*

Three times Grand National winner, Red Rum, was a global superstar, and a king of steeplechasers. Like that other great chaser,

Desert Orchid, he epitomised the extraordinary courage and allure of horses. This is a story about our own equine stars, and the spunk of their riders. A story of exhilaration in the heated cauldron of competition. It is about looking forward with optimism, and the benefit of hindsight. Sporting ambition had weaved a clear passage through my life. I occasionally ask myself, 'Would I do it again? Would I do things differently?' Perhaps my story will reveal the answers.

Some of our horses became champions and winners. Others – quite a few – did not. They had their own stories to tell. But they had four legs, they couldn't speak, so I listened to a voice in my head and in my heart and knew that I did not want those stories to disappear, that I must record them, for my family, for all horse lovers, and for everyone who likes a challenge, whatever it may be. You may shed a tear and, I hope, smile a bit too.

But first I must go back to the early days, to eventual achievement from unlikely beginnings, and create a picture of the background to those stories; to the impossible dreams held by a child of nine with only one thing on her mind – to own a pony to care for, to talk to, and to love.

ONE

THE PASSION – EARLY CHILDHOOD IN EGYPT

I longed, no, I yearned to own a pony. The sight of them stirred me. It was their powerful sense of freedom – of grace, speed and fire. I thought they were such wondrous creatures with their flowing manes and tails, and large luminous eyes. I wanted to stroke them, feel their warm coats and most of all to ride them, and borrow that speed, hear the beat of thudding hooves drumming in my ears, thrill to the cold wind rushing past my face. But I was raised in what is known as a non-horsey background – a rather sniffy term for a 'townie'. Living in the countryside meant a landscape of meadows, mountains and moors. I had read stories by the Pullein-Thompson sisters about going hunting and galloping up hills and down vales, following the cry of a pack of hounds. I wanted to explore the mystery of remote places, and was fascinated by the creatures of the night that lived there – the wily fox, the mythical hare, Brock the badger and others. Riding ponies and the countryside seemed to dovetail together, but I was going to have to wait for a long time, and childhood soon passed by. The longing, however, never went away.

I had barely sat on a pony, let alone owned one. We were a British family living in Egypt, in the smart suburb of Zamalek, outside Cairo, surrounded by sand, pyramids and the majestic River Nile. I should mention here that the following brief description of our life in Egypt in the 1950s may bear no resemblance to the country today.

My father was with Shell Oil, and my mother enjoyed the ex-pat life of tennis, bridge and parties. I had ridden camels in the desert and gazed, with a sense of adoration, at the Arabian horses in the enclosed grounds of the Pasha's house opposite our apartment and at the polo ponies, dashing like lightning across the glowing green grass of the Gezira Sporting Club, where suffragies – native servants – balanced trays above the neat, white turbans on their heads, and weaved expertly between chattering tables crowded with British army officers, diplomats, bankers, employees of the oil companies and their wives.

The Gezira Sporting Club was exclusive, and there remained a defined social stratum as there had been when the club was launched in 1883 by the British army, when only officers were accepted. Egyptians without influence were also barred. Egypt was a British Protectorate, but the power of the Empire was still in evidence. I swam in the sparkling blue pool, drank Coca Cola, and ate peanuts – you needed the salt. Sometimes we went for family picnics with friends into the desert at night amongst the ancient tombs, the sky an inky blue and studded with twinkling stars. Ponies and green fields were just in those story books and thousands of miles away in another land.

Cairo was a cosmopolitan, multi faith city teeming with Egyptians, Turks, Moslems, Jews and Greeks. Car horns blared continuously – the noise was deafening; trams rattled past, heaving with native men and boys, leaning out and hanging from the open doors. Donkey carts, mules and street traders crowded the streets, and bartered in the colourful mouski (market place). Women shrouded in black remained in the villages, just their eyes visible, gazing secretly through the slit of the customary veil. Their feet were bare and dusty, while ragged children clutched their skirts, and babies, eyes encrusted black with crawling flies, clung to swaying hips. The heat was stifling, and smells from spicy cooking, animals, no sanitation and warm dried dung – much of it used to cook with, pervaded the air. More children followed, small brown hands outstretched for baksheesh. 'Imshi, imshi,' my mother would say, hurrying on. Here were mud huts, goats, scraggy hens, and camels lying on the earth-caked roads. Flies buzzed and droned.

This was the fellaheen, the archetypal peasant. Poverty was rife. There were beggars everywhere, all the time, some crippled and pulling themselves along on makeshift wheeled planks. Donkeys laden with heavy burdens tittupped along, just the tips of their grey ears visible, as boys pushed and nagged them with sticks. Mangy, starving dogs sometimes found their way to our residential area. Animals in distress had always upset me. This was a side of Egypt we rarely saw, and a far cry from the boulevards of Zamalek, trailing with pink and white bougainvillea, and where drinks arrived at sundown.

Shepheard's Hotel in the city hosted social gatherings amongst its marbled terraces, orchestra and fringed palms, or you could have tea at Groppi's cafe with its exotic sweetmeats and cakes. Everywhere – wealthy or poor – the great River Nile flowed, the life force and heartbeat of this ancient country. Feluccas drifted lazily along the river, sweeping sails billowing gently in the breeze, and along the banks stood the flat-roofed white houses and the domes of the mosques, while the hot yellow sand undulated and stretched into the shimmering haze beyond. As darkness fell, the eerie sound of wailing could be heard across the city, as the mandatory prayers to Allah echoed into the night.

British people in Cairo kept well up to date with events in the UK. It was February 6th 1952, and there was an agitated stir of disbelief. The sudden death of King George V1 had been announced that morning.

The King is dead, the King is dead. Those words resonate still.

The loss of a king, who had been a figure of strength throughout the war years, was a profound shock to UK citizens out in Egypt.

British Cairo led a charmed life, but it was to change.

Unrest among the native people churned, and trouble brewed as resentment against the corrupt Egyptian King Farouk, and the power of the British, grew. We were advised not to speak English in the city, and my mother spoke French, in which she was fluent. Egypt erupted into civil war. With terrifying speed the centre of Cairo was ablaze. A murky dim haze crept across the vivid blue sky, and hot orange spread like liquid as Cairo burnt. The rabble headed to the city in open trucks, guns held above their heads. My father had gone to Cairo that morning as usual, but the mob was torching everything British, including Shepheard's Hotel and the Shell building. He and his colleagues escaped with their loyal Egyptian chauffeur, who drove them dashing through the back streets, wearing borrowed tarbooshes – red fezzes.

Shell evacuated wives and children swiftly. I sat by the little window of our BOAC aeroplane and waved to my father as we taxied down the Cairo runway to the safety of England. We would soon be enveloped in the excitement of Queen Elizabeth II's glittering coronation in 1953, and the conquest of Mount Everest for the first time, by New Zealander Edmund Hillary with his Tibetan guide, Tenzing. In 1954, British athlete Roger Bannister broke a record, and ran a mile in four minutes.

My father had lived in the searing heat of both the Far and the Middle East all his working life, but now a career with champagne producers G H Mumm & Co., in Liverpool, awaited him. The three day race meeting of the Grand National retained a race called the Mumm Melling Chase up until the year 2000, no doubt in association with the drinks company, Seagrams, the sponsors of the Grand National. The north of England was unknown territory for us. The long leaves my father and family took from Shell every two years in the UK were spent in Devon, or in Cornwall on the edge of Bodmin Moor. But it was the convenient Cheshire town of Hoylake, on the Wirral peninsula, where we settled. The golf and tennis clubs were nearby, and the commuter train snaked its way beneath the River Mersey to the city of Liverpool.

The River Mersey has one of the most impressive waterfronts in the world, dominated in those days by the Liver Building, the Cunard Building and the Port of Liverpool Building – known collectively as The Three Graces. Erected at the beginning of the 20th century, these majestic structures were striking evidence of the commercial strength of Liverpool at that time. This was a city fuelled by great wealth from shipping, cotton, sugar, grain and the slave trade. As the crow flies, Hoylake is not so far away from the home of the Grand National – Aintree racecourse.

The town looks over the River Dee estuary towards the Irish Sea, and is situated on the south side of the Wirral. On the north side is the dockside town of Birkenhead, which rolls on into the smoke and flame spewing chemical refineries and oil tanks of Ellesmere Port. In the 14th century Hoylake was a seafaring hamlet, home to sailors and fishermen. Ships from Ireland landed sheep and cattle which travelled by drove to Chester.

Hoylake retains two significant places of interest. Gulls scream and swoop over a wide road lined with commodious houses near the sea shore, called King's Gap. Named thus, because in 1690 it was from Hoylake – the Hoyle Lake – that King William of Orange set up camp and sailed across the Irish Sea, to face the Stuart King James II at the Battle of the Boyne. Thousands of the king's horses and troops had left six months earlier in preparation for battle. They too sailed from Hoylake. One of those horses on the heaving boats was known as the Byerley Turk, a horse who was to carve himself a place in history as the first of the three foundation sires of today's thoroughbred racehorse, and whose blood pounds across British turf every day of the week.

The second place of note is the Royal Liverpool golf course, usually called just 'Hoylake' by golfing pundits, and site of the Open Championships first held there in 1897. But there is racing history connected to Hoylake, because in the middle of the 19th century the golf course began as a racecourse. Horse-drawn omnibuses arrived from Birkenhead, picking up passengers off the Mersey ferry from Liverpool, and dropping them off at the Green Lodge Hotel in Hoylake, which is still there today. Hunting enthusiast Sir William Stanley originally owned the course, and kept a pack of foxhounds near Willaston, on the Wirral. The course was eventually purchased by the Liverpool Hunt Club. There was even hunting on the outskirts of Liverpool in those far off days.

Today there is a recognisable racing name amongst the club's elite, listed on the oak-panelled walls of the Royal Liverpool Golf Club, and that is Sangster. Vernon Sangster, a former captain of the club, with his wife Margaret – known as Peggy – and their son Robert, lived in one of the many fine houses situated on Meols Drive in Hoylake, known locally as 'millionaires mile'. Robert Sangster became the owner of two Derby winners, with The Minstrel and Golden Fleece, three l'Arc de Triomphes, plus many other classics, his horses often ridden by Lester Piggott. He created the Coolmore Stud in County Tipperary, Southern Ireland, with John Magnier and Vincent O'Brien. The Coolmore Stud carries on the racing tradition today, in association with the enigmatic and brilliant Ballydoyle trainer, Aidan O'Brien – although no relation to Vincent.

Sangster was a powerful name in Wirral circles, due to Robert's racing accolades, and principally to the success of his father's business empire, Vernon's Football Pools, which had created immense wealth. Peggy Sangster was proud of her son's (Robert was an only child) racing achievements, and enjoyed talking about them round the bridge table. Grace always watched the racing on television looking for the familiar green and blue Sangster colours. Peggy admired my mother, who was a good bridge player, but Peggy sometimes became a little imperious – particularly after a large gin or two; but Grace was never daunted by her, as some were.

After they both became widowed they enjoyed jaunts together. When my mother ceased driving, having written off her car, which was a relief to all other road users, Peggy kindly sent the Rolls plus liveried chauffeur to collect Grace for many a bridge afternoon. Mother spent some days on the Isle of Man at Robert's house, The Nunnery, with Peggy. She described to me the meticulous graphs of breeding stock, and the hundreds of horses owned by Robert, all immaculately displayed and itemised on the extensive walls of the lower ground floor of The Nunnery. Astute enough to realise that, despite his own great wealth, when the oil-rich Arabs became involved with flat racing Robert could not compete in the sale ring. He continued with the breeding of classic winners. The great horse Sadlers Wells was owned by Robert, and has left his legacy at stud through his son Galileo, the outstanding stallion of the present time, and sire of Frankel.

Peggy invited Grace to dine with her on occasions, sometimes at Claridges or in the red and gold opulence of the Ritz restaurant with its twinkling chandeliers. Royal fashion designer Sir Norman Hartnell, also dining one evening, spotted his client and made his way ever so graciously to Peggy's table, gave a little bow, and said, 'My dear Mrs Sangster, I see we are wearing the blue this evening,' implying he had seen his creation worn before, and it was about time she ordered another!

My father had a mischievous sense of humour, and liked to invent names for Grace's bridge ladies. Emboldened by his usual tipple, and referring to a lady of a pit bull nature – especially around the bridge table – he would call out, 'It's the Old Trout on the phone – are you in?'

He was more polite when Peggy Sangster rang; 'It's for you – it's Lady Bootle.'

Those familiar with the city of Liverpool in those days would know that Bootle, in Liverpool, was an area where the police only patrolled in multiples.

Situated in a quiet tree-lined road, within walking distance of the beach and the Royal Liverpool Golf Club, where both my parents played golf, our house was one of many of the late Victorian and Edwardian era. Our only association with horses were family outings into the Cheshire countryside for the annual point-to-point races and, on my father's insistence, this included a favourite venue of his, Mucklestone in Staffordshire.

So here we were in England, the green and pleasant land of contented cows, and horses grazing in grassy meadows as far as the eye could see, far away from the dust and heat of Egypt. I imagined a drive up to a house with paddocks on either side. 'Room for a pony', as Hyacinth Bucket would say. There would be hills to gallop across, winding rivers, woods to explore, and lambs playing in the fields around, a rural idyll. But not a bit of it – I was to be confined to the convenience of suburbia. Everywhere I looked I saw brick and asphalt. Pavements studded with trim trees, methodically spaced. Rows of detached houses called Mountview, Ingledene or The Gables. Bus stops, and manicured flower beds. So instead, every Saturday, attired in twill jodhpurs, a yellow polo-necked sweater and brown lace-up shoes, I jumped onto a green Crosville bus with a velvet peaked riding hat under my arm, sandwiches made by my father stuffed into my pocket, and my bus fare. Leaping up the spiral staircase, I gazed through the window of the top deck with vacant disinterest as the bus trundled its way through the red roofs of the Wirral towns of West Kirby, Frankby and Upton. In half an hour I perked up. I had reached my destination. Arrowe Park Riding School.

Climbing the great stack of hay and straw, and heaving down the heavy bales, was fun. I quite liked the pungent smell of the steaming muck heap because it meant ponies. In the tack room, dusty grey cobwebs floated across the ceiling, and a jumble of saddles, bridles, dandy brushes, curry combs, and bars of slippery saddle soap were strewn across trunks, chests of drawers, and wooden saddle horses, while the more pleasant and homely aromas of well-used leather, pots of sticky hoof oil, Stockholm tar, and boiled barley popping and bubbling on a rusty stove, enveloped me with a contented feeling of what I loved most – yes, ponies. There were bins of oats and bran, shovels, forks and rickety barrows. I mucked out, swept the cobbled yard with a stiff broom taller than myself, brushed tangled manes, tails and forelocks, bumped around a puddled sand arena on a mixture of ordinary ponies, and sat on the straw bales eating my sandwiches with horse hair clinging to my clothes, and probably with very grimy hands too. It was all wonderful.

At 4pm, happy, with mud on my shoes and straw stuck to my yellow jersey, I caught the bus back to Hoylake. Reluctant to arrive home too soon, I skipped up and down the road in a canter-like gait, jumping on and off the pavement while clicking to an imaginary pony and flicking the air with my riding whip. Once home, for the rest of that day and the next, I refused to wash. Horses have a distinctive smell. Part sweat, part meadow and sweet hay, part hoof when the farrier singes the foot for shoeing, part the soft air they blow into your face, and probably part dung too. It is warm and velvety like their muzzles. For me, as a pony addict, it was a glorious, evocative scent; it would be another week before I could be with my four-legged companions again, and I wanted to put my unwashed hands up to my nose, breathe it in for as long as I possibly could, and go to bed with it.

One day, I ran home from the bus and announced there was to be a local show near the riding school, and a few children could enter with the riding school ponies. My pony was Dandy. He was the plainest little chap possible, a washy chestnut with a large docile head, a mane that fell thickly on both sides of his stumpy neck, and clumps of feather round his ponderous hooves. With the help of my friends, I did my best to smarten up Dandy, and chopped the feather on his heels. I was hoping to ride a pretty black pony called Dazzle, who was actually a little witch, and would lash out with a hind leg when you entered her stable, and then cart you bucketing across the field with her ears between her knees, but we had drawn lots, so that was that.

Excitedly, four children, including myself, clip clopped the half mile along the road to the show. Our class was called, and I spotted my parents watching at the side of the roped off arena. I slotted in amongst the string of children and ponies nose to tail, about three feet apart. In the middle was a corpulent lady wrapped in a tweed skirt and a matching jacket stretched tight across the twin peaks of her ample chest. She was the judge. A felt hat tipped forward on her head and a cheeky feather waved from the hat band. As she watched us, legs planted firmly apart, she masterfully managed to twizzle round on her shooting stick, while her posterior spilled impressively over both sides of the small leather seat. Standing beside her was a ring steward in a hacking jacket, wittering over a clipboard with a bunch of rosettes clutched in her hand.

Some of the ponies were plaited and polished, and ridden by experienced children buffed up in navy jackets, sitting with stiff backs and ramrod arms, but I hardly had a chance to notice. Before completing even one circuit of the arena the steward had waved me in first, and then, one by one, my companions from the riding school, and a couple of others. Goodness, there I was standing at the head of the line. I saw my parents smiling at me. Had my undoubted talent been spotted by this very important person in the middle of the arena? Then, as the flood of excitement had childishly welled up, it vanished into pathetic obscurity, like a worm squirming in the mud. I and the other five children standing beside me were asked to leave the arena, as we were no longer required – and we hadn't even progressed into a trot.

Looking back it is really very funny, but at the time I burned with humiliation and indignation, as I turned plain little Dandy away, and left the arena with the others. It was the first time, and the last for many years, that I would enter another pony show ring. Purchased by Lord Leverhulme from a Liverpool ship owner, the land at Arrowe Park is now a public park. The riding school is a pub called The Stirrup, and the field where we rode and the ponies grazed is a modern estate of identical brick houses, which sprawls into the conurbation and dockside town of Birkenhead on the River Mersey. That experience, at the age of ten, sowed a seed, which spurred me on to events in the years that followed, which I could not possibly have imagined at that time, and which I will describe in the following chapters.

Some years had passed since my days at the riding school. It was now the Swinging Sixties. Britain was sparking, and the greyness had been replaced by a new vibrancy. The universe had survived the nuclear threat of the Cuban crisis in 1962, and news the following year that Jack Kennedy, better known as JFK – the American president – had been assassinated, shocked the world. Mini-skirts and attempting to look like model Jean Shrimpton was the fashion, something called 'the Pill' had been invented, and a rock band of floppy-haired Merseyside boys was about to become famous in a Liverpool cellar called The Cavern. I was married, to Liverpool solicitor Christopher Lyon, and living in the pretty, semi-rural village of Burton on the edge of the Wirral. One day I casually noticed an advertisement in the local Chester and North Wales newspaper under 'Livestock'.

Welsh X Arab pony. 12.2hh. 3 years old. Unbroken. North Wales.

I set off into rolling hills, drove up a hedge-lined farm track, and parked beside a low, whitewashed stone farmhouse, with a small corrugated roofed stable attached at one end. The farmer, with a Welsh collie running close to his heels, greeted me affably, touching his cap. He picked up a rope halter hanging on a rusty nail jutting from the wall of the stable, and out from the dark came the prettiest pony imaginable. She was a deep dusky palomino colour with a silvery white mane and tail, which flowed long and wispy. She had a neat dished face – meaning concave, typical of Welsh Mountain ponies and Arab horses, and large brown eyes. Here was the dream pony and at last I could have it. I handed twenty-five pounds to my Welsh friend, and as I did so he pulled out a crumpled ten shilling note from his pocket, turned my palm up, slapped it quite firmly, and then pressed the note into my hand. I looked at him, surprised. Had I given him the wrong money? But a smile creased across his weather-lined face.

'Luck money, cariad,' (Welsh for 'my dear') he said in a lilting voice.

I discovered that luck money is an age-old custom amongst gypsies and country dwellers, and seen at livestock auctions and horse fairs, like Appleby in the Lake District. Perhaps a little of that luck would pop up in the years to come.

I called the pony Heidi, after a favourite family dachshund. I broke her in using instinct and a 'how to' book, and led her with a head collar and rope like a pet dog, while together we ambled happily along the lanes around Burton, and then one day I leant across her, and sat on her bare back. The Welsh are pony show enthusiasts, and soon I found a show near the Clwydian hills in the village of Cilcaen. I entered Heidi for the in hand Mountain and Moorland class so the ponies did not require plaiting, which was just as well, as I had no clue how to produce those neatly sewn rosebuds.

About twenty ponies were led round the arena, and one by one we came into the centre and did our practised show. I stood my little pony up in front of the judge – a respected breeder of Welsh ponies. He was leanly-built, and wore a tweed jacket patched with leather at the elbows, which hung loosely from his shoulders, and rather a battered bowler hat. He leant on his thumb stick, and looked keenly with sharp blue eyes. Each pony was scrutinised and we trotted round again for a final judging. A decision was made. The judge tipped his bowler hat and walked straight towards Heidi and me, holding out his hand. I was presented with a cup and a bright red rosette which fluttered gaily on Heidi's bridle. Behind the ropes stood Christopher, smiling broadly, with a small Tory in a pushchair, and beside her was Kerry, our black and white spaniel. This was a rustic show on the side of a Welsh mountain, with sheep bleating, cows mooing, simple country folk, muddied Land-Rovers and farm trailers parked haphazardly. It was also my first taste of a red rosette – and of winning. It was a thrilling feeling.

My pony Heidi fanned the flame of many more pony and horse purchases, and over fifty years, and still learning, I experienced through ignorance and on the job, so to speak; crib biters, wind suckers, weavers – nervous habits; sweet itch, spavins, pedalosteitis – a serious inflammation of the pedal bone in the foot, which Red Rum suffered from, and was cured by his trainer, Ginger McCain, galloping him through the cooling salt waters of Southport beach. I discovered nappy horses, fired horses, worms, kissing spines, head shakers, whistlers and roarers, and parrot mouths – an overshot upper jaw, which Red Rum also had. I will avoid explaining the intricacies of all these undesirable horse afflictions, but horse people will recognise them. Training horses successfully, in whatever discipline, is a melting pot of complexities. They never cease to challenge us, and will often turn every known theory upside down.

At last I had my pony, and now too, the house with paddocks that was so set in my mind as a child. That image had never gone away, and when the bailiff's house to Burton Manor came on the market, Christopher wasted no time. Burton Manor had been owned by the family of William Gladstone, and the bailiff's house – called The Chase, due to a fox earth in the orchard – was built of red Cheshire sandstone, and surrounded by woodland, orchard and fields. Trees overhung the drive, and wild daffodils and bluebells grew in profusion in the wooded area to the right. The estate parkland adjoined and continued down to woods, a hidden lake and the Burton marshes.

In the far distance, and over the River Dee estuary, was the John Summers steel works at Shotton in North Wales. At night, when lit up with eruptions of orange flame, sparks and muffled bangs, this huge industrial site contrasted dramatically with the wild expanse of the sedge-covered marshes, with its wading and migrating bird population. If you picked your way, avoiding the water-filled gullies, you could ride a horse to Ness further along the marshes – which Christopher occasionally did, calling in for a pint at the remote Harp Inn. From there the estuary continues up to Parkgate, once a busy fishing port, and birth place of Horatio Nelson's mistress, Emma Hamilton, the local blacksmith's daughter.

Anxious to improve my equine knowledge and limited riding ability, I travelled daily to the Wirral Riding Centre at Ness, enrolling myself on a British Horse Society Instructor's qualification, which I managed to scrape through. Tory was packed off to nursery in nearby Willaston, and Polly to Mrs Jones, the farmer's wife, in the village. I immersed myself with huge enthusiasm into the twelve month full-time course, which was led by Geoffrey Hatton FBHS –Fellow of the British Horse Society. He was an austere figure, and with few words. Quite short in stature, he always wore dark glasses, cavalry twill breeches, and a bomber type jacket of shiny, black leather, which issued a sort of squeak, squeak, squeak, in time with his step, as he strode around the indoor riding school in tan-topped riding boots – with spurs. I was rather frightened of him, but at last I was learning about horses, and every day was a fulfilment; the riding especially, but also the theory and practice of horse management, and the skill of first aid veterinary practice. Nothing replaces experience, but at least I had made a start, and I loved it.

Soon I turned my attention to ponies for our daughters, Tory and Polly. Ian was a black Dartmoor pony with a white star. He was ancient and safe, and came to us from Tory's best friend Fenella Fawcus. Fenella and her pony Dewdrop would often stay with us overnight. Early one morning I was woken by noises coming from outside. Peering through the window in a cold misty dawn, I saw two small girls, aged six and seven, in the paddock below. One pony was half tacked up with its head in a bucket, and the other was trotting triumphantly round the field with a rope trailing behind him, refusing to be caught. Then I noticed the children still had on their pyjamas. I shrugged and went back to bed. They had, after all, remembered to put on their jodhpur boots, and hard hats.

We joined the Burton Cheshire Forest branch of the Pony Club, which is based on the Wirral. The Cheshire Forest hounds and the Royal Rock beagles – the oldest pack of beagles in the country – originally hunted on the Wirral, but both ceased to do so due to urbanisation and persecution by the countryside pest, the 'animal rights' movement and the hunt saboteurs. The Pony Club is the largest equestrian youth organisation in the world. Founded in 1929 by members of local hunts for the benefit of farmers' and subscribers' children. In 1930 there were 300 members. Currently there are approximately 50,000 members and around 345 branches throughout Britain.

We had so much carefree fun in those days. Tory moved on to Crispy, a sassy palomino pony purchased from Jenny Loriston-Clarke, and Polly, rode Ian. Our Pony Club friends were the Jackson girls, Gail and Clare, with their lovely black pony, Magic, Zoe Hancox and her roly-poly chestnut pony, Impy, and the Lloyd boys with their pony, Jack. Crispy, young and bright, proved a challenge for Tory, particularly as she had an arm in a sling with a broken collar bone. Every afternoon after school, we hacked to the fields and marshes, and while I kept a constant eye on the sharp Crispy, Polly aged four and the one-paced Ian did their own thing. Every so often I looked back to check they were still with us, and with legs flapping against the ageing pony's sides, I could hear 'Go on Red Rum, go on Red Rum'. She was quite happy, riding the most famous steeplechaser of the era.

There was an extensive badger sett in the woods below our house. I had noticed it on our rides with the ponies. Living in Egypt and Hoylake, I had never seen a badger, and one spring, Christopher and I set off at dusk to see if we could spot the cubs playing outside their home. Wearing dark clothes and carrying a torch we made our way to the woods. It was chilly and we huddled behind a tree, a little way from one of the many exits of the sett. Badgers keep their homes very clean, and we chose a deep hole that had clearly been used, as there was debris and leaves outside, and the grass was trodden down. I felt a quiet excitement. The secret life of nocturnal wild animals I find magical and mysterious.

We waited – but not for long. Soon there was a rustle, and then a shiny black nose peeked out and wriggled as it sniffed the air. Through the trees, the dark earth streaked with moonlight I saw a big badger followed by the cubs. They tumbled and rolled and nipped each other. We must have watched for about twenty minutes before they returned underground, and the adult lumbered off to hunt for food. Nearly forty-five years since that sighting, I revisited those woods, and still as active as ever is that badger sett. The woodland and the marshes beyond are now part of a protected wild fowl centre known as Burton Mere.

Sadly, badgers have become a controversial issue. Much as I love to see them, some farmers are having an impossibly difficult time, with their livelihoods threatened by bovine TB, which is carried by badgers. Conservation and preserving our native wildlife is vital, but you cannot be sentimental. Knowledgeable management is the key to keeping a successful balance for badgers and many more of our indigenous British species, which include red squirrels and water voles, overpowered by the dominant grey squirrel and voracious mink. True countrymen are the best people to decide how this should be achieved. They understand the countryside as a working environment – not as a theme park. Sometimes the BBC wildlife and countryside programmes on television come over as rather too cosy.

TWO

WALES – THE PULL OF THE HILLS, AND A HOUSE CALLED PEN PARC LLWYD

'Do you know the Tilleys?' my friend Mary Fawcus asked me one day. I was looking for a horse for myself.

'No – should I?' I said.

'Well, everyone knows the Tilleys, give them a ring – ask for Daphne.'

And with that I made a call to the Tilley family, farmers and horse dealers in Denbighshire, North Wales. 'I know of just the animal,' said Daphne Tilley down the phone.

'He belongs to Trefor Eames, the blacksmith, and is a 'very nice stamp'. We are off to Badminton tomorrow, but do come and see the horse when we get back.'

Badminton is the Cheltenham Gold Cup of eventing. Olympic and world class riders compete in the splendour of the Duke of Beaufort's estate in Gloucestershire. I had never been and I listened impressed, but it was some months later that I set off for the village of Henllan, near Denbigh, and the Tilleys' farmhouse, Pen Parc Llwyd – the White House in the Park.

In the early 1970s this part of North Wales was predominately sheep farms and Welsh black cattle, which are small and hardy like the Welsh sheep. Ponies bred on the farm were often used by farmers to round up the flock from the hills. They were strong and able to carry weight. There were some notable Welsh pony breeders in North Wales at that time, among them the Coed Coch stud situated in the hills behind the sea. The house was later to become Heronwater prep school. The first language of many of the farming, and local community was Welsh, and perhaps still is. The busy market town of Denbigh, with its ancient Norman castle set high on a crag, is three miles away, but once out of the town, driving west towards the moors, the countryside becomes increasingly bleak, treeless and remote. Beyond that is Snowdonia, one of the wildest parts of Britain. It is here the Eryri hounds meet and hunt. They are a foot pack, as the area is too treacherous to hunt on horseback. One New Year's day we met at The Sportsmans Arms, high on the Denbigh moors – now sadly closed. Trying to keep up with hounds was almost impossible as they leapt up and down boulders, and disappeared into gulleys and dense covert. Welsh hounds are independent and will often hunt on their own. The hills of North Wales are majestic, forbidding and stunningly beautiful at different times of the year. The villages built from grey stone and slate were spartan.

As I drove through Henllan, small children played in the road unconcerned, sheep grazed on the grass verges, and chickens pecked and scratched about in the dust. There was very little traffic. A pretty stone church – St. Sadwrn – stood on a hillock, and below was a line of terraced cottages. A farmer leant idly on the fence, a curl of smoke rising from his pipe, and beside him on the rough stone wall stretched a black and white sheepdog. An old grey tractor took up most of the small yard of his cottage. As I drove past, I was aware of him eyeing the car under his oil stained cap. Any unfamiliar vehicle was noticed. I experienced a strange but distinct sensation of driving through a past century. It seemed a long way from the familiar predictability of the Wirral that I was used to. It never crossed my mind that one day I might be living in this village up in the hills of North Wales.

My first impression of Willy Tilley was of a large ebullient character. As joint master of the local pack of foxhounds, a heavyweight hunter, or two, was therefore essential to carry his ample frame whilst leading the field across the hills and vales of the Flint and Denbigh Hunt country. I bumped down the stony farm drive, and round the corner came Daphne. In contrast to Willy she is the opposite of tall, and was completely dwarfed by a pair of giant horses towering above her, one on either side, which she was leading with head collars. These were Willy's hunters. A Roman-nosed chestnut, with a bold expression, and a flea-bitten (meaning spotted) grey with lop ears and hooves the size of dinner plates. A Roman nose, in reference to a horse, is the opposite of dished or concave, and usually denotes a touch of the cart or draught in the breeding. However, many horses like this show great character, and courage too. Daphne, attired in generous brown corduroys and boots, strode towards me with her equine charges. With a mane of wavy hair flying in the wind, she called out, 'Welcome to Pen Parc. I will be with you in a moment.'

Used to keeping puckish children under orders in the Pony Club, the echoes of Daphne's voice could be heard in the next county, and possibly even beyond. She was affectionately known as 'Dumpy' by Willy. Driving into the stable yard there were horses and ponies poking their heads out of every conceivable farm building, of which there were many. I parked the car and was greeted by Willy.

'Come in, come in,' he hailed.

Stepping over several dozing cats and a hen in the stone porch, I followed him into a beamed room. A smoky film hung in the air, and there was a pleasant woody smell drifting from the smouldering logs, which sparked and glowed in an open hearth. The room was liberally hung with greenery – holly, fir and mistletoe, as it was Christmas time, and a large cake, covered in white icing rising in frosty peaks, sat on the oak dresser. A Christmas tree, lit-up with multi-coloured lights, stood cheerfully in the corner. Willy had recently returned from hunting in Leicestershire, and as I settled myself into a capacious and sagging armchair, a small smiling girl – Lavinia, the younger Tilley daughter – handed me a piece of cake and a cup of lukewarm, milky tea. I picked out a few cat's hairs floating on the top, and listened as Willy regaled the pleasures of hunting in the shires. This, he said, with a twinkle in his eye, included a comely little number riding side saddle, who tittupped over on a smart dapple grey.

Time passed but there was no sign of Daphne. I noticed through the window a constant traffic of horse boxes, trailers, ponies and children. Shouts echoed outside.

'Have you fed Marmite? Don't forget to clean your tack before you go home, Fenella. Has Monty been skipped out?' Plus the clippity clop of hooves, whinnies and children's chatter, and still there was no sign of Daphne. People popped their heads round the door in greeting, and I was introduced impressively by Willy as having come over from Cheshire and looking for a good hunter.

An hour started to become two, and just as I was beginning to think the horse did not exist, Daphne blew in, apologised profusely, and grabbing my riding hat I was bundled out of the house and into a cranking maroon Rover plastered with mud. Easing myself into the shiny leather passenger seat, creased with age and peppered with hay and horse nuts, I landed with a bump to the hard floor of the car. A pug dog jumped in, snuffled and grunted like a pig, turned itself round and round on Daphne's knee, and we were off, jolting up the drive and into the hills, to view the horse. Pulling into a small stable yard with a forge in an open barn, I could make out a dark bay head over a stable door, in the now fading December light. However, there was no sign of Trefor Eames; more apologies from Daphne.

'Dooo come and have a day's hunting, and then you can try the horse properly. We have a lawn meet at Pen Parc in a fortnight. There will be a good crowd out.'

About two years later, I did return to Henllan, but not to buy a horse. This time it was with Christopher to look at a house which was on the market. I knew the house; I had been there before – it was Pen Parc Llwyd. Willy and Daphne and their five children, Tuffy, John, Lavinia, David and Dicka, had ventured into the country house hotel business. They had purchased Galtfaenan Hall, which is Grade Two listed, surrounded by parkland and situated in the best part of the Flint and Denbigh Hunt country known as The Vale. Here, along with the Fawcus family, they planned to run residential hunting holidays and pony camps. As prospective purchasers of their house, Willy and Daphne had invited us for Sunday lunch.

Driving into the farm yard at Pen Parc once more, we were met by a large goose strutting stiff-legged in the manner of Hitler's SS. Trotting behind him on her little cloven hooves came a lone sheep, her fleece bouncing like a thick blanket around her. This was Flossie, the family pet. 'B-a-a-a' she said in a deep throaty voice, staring at us with pale straw-coloured eyes. Willy emerged with a terrier darting between his heels, and a second goose padded over on her orange feet and joined the welcome party. Willy then led us, picking our way through the slosh of the muddy yard, to 'take a butchers' at the farm buildings before viewing the house. Rupert, the goose, tucked close to his heels, hissed angrily.

'Oh! worry not,' boomed Willy, 'he's my best friend, take no notice. He hasn't goosed anyone for ages. The last time was Huge-gin, a week ago,' Whereupon he scooped up the honking bird, and dropped him with a flourish into the trickling stream nearby.

Willy was well known for his nicknames, and the bearer of this cheeky one was a noble lady in the area, whose correct name was Hugelin – pronounced with a hard G. Unperturbed, Rupert reappeared, shook himself vigorously, covering us with sprays of water, stretched up his head importantly, and placed himself once again between his master and us. Arriving at the house, there again in the stone porch, with just a twitch of an ear, and a blink of an amber eye, were the sleepy cats, stretched out like a furry rug of tabby, tortoiseshell, and marmalade.

Pushing open the door Willy led us into the kitchen. A meaty aroma wafted from the solid bulk of the Aga cooker, which dominated one end of the room. Noticeably burnt-stained with much use, this stuttering, coke fuelled, cream-coloured old stove would now be considered a period piece. Drying over the metal bar in front dangled several string girths, and an earthy reek of animals, particularly horse, twitched my nose. On the boarded floor in the corner, waiting to be cleaned, lay a pile of tack, glistening wet and sweaty, with the familiar orange bar of saddle soap nearby. Displayed above the Aga hung an array of rosettes – red, blue, green, yellow, etc., along with faded black and white photographs of hunting scenes, and men at horse shows in bowler hats. Scrawled on the wall by the phone was a list of names and numbers. The vet, the blacksmith, the animal feed merchant, the hunt kennels – didn't notice the doctor, though!

The room was akin to livestock market day in Denbigh. A noisy stream of animals and people coming and going, it bubbled with activity. Children trotted in and out, tousle-haired, bits of straw clinging to their clothes, and wearing jodhpurs which were none too clean. When remembered, boots were left in a muddy jumble in the porch. The cats sloped in, and Flossie too, if she had half a chance. Tuffy, thirteen years old with a mop of curly hair, was the eldest Tilley child, and seemed to be in charge of the riding, while Lavinia stood on a stable bucket with her hands in a high stone sink doing the washing up. The visiting kids, staying the week with their ponies, were having the time of their lives. Sleeping dormitory fashion in the far end of the house, they were bright-eyed and rosy-cheeked from riding across the hills and vales, wind through their hair, sun and rain on their faces, grooming, mucking out, and generally running pretty wild. Not much sign of the dreaded 'elf-n-safety' here.

In North Wales, sheep were the main source of farming income, and in the top oven of the Aga sizzled our lunch, which, of course, was roast lamb. On the floor close to the Aga nestled a pair of orphan lambs, their woolly faces peeping under a dark grey ex-army blanket edged with red stitching. Every now and then, one lifted its head and gave a pathetic little bleat. *'M-a-a-a.'* Nearby, for the lambs, there stood a baby bottle of milk. A large pinewood table was laid up, and the meal was a movable feast. The farmworker, Phil, and grooms, Barbara and Helen, soon arrived, interspersed with hungry children.

As the meal progressed and the port arrived with the Stilton, Willy – quite a raconteur – got into his stride, leant back, large boots on the chair opposite, and regaled us with a story or two, perhaps embroidered somewhat. This one entailed a group of young army recruits who were on manoeuvres on the moors around Denbigh. The route took them through the top farmyard at Pen Parc. Now Willy's philosophy in life could be described as hunting and the good life, convivial company, and all that went with it. Animals abounded everywhere, and there was plenty of muck and mud, along with a conglomeration of abandoned cars in the quarry behind the barns. Shovelling shit and keeping a spick and span farmyard did not appear to be high on the list.

Willy's story went something like this.

'The troops came jogging over the hill towards Pen Parc with their kit on their backs. An officer with a map in his hand called out, "Come on now, chaps, onward ahead," and this they did, whereupon there erupted yells of disgust and the air turned blue, as the lads disappeared up to their waists, squelching, slithering and floundering in evil-smelling liquid, hidden beneath a layer of verdant green grass. Of course, if I had known they were going that way, I would have warned them that I hadn't emptied that slurry tip for months. Their language was absolutely appalling.'

As this story unravelled, Daphne appeared with a third lamb. Tiny and weak, it was placed in the bottom oven of the Aga on a towel, while its damp, fleecy sides, moving faintly in and out, were just discernible through the open door. In sheep country this was not an unusual sight, and one I was to witness again in the stone farmhouse at Bryn-Rhyd-y-Arian, up in the hills where the Tilleys later lived, although that time I think it might have been kittens. Willy, by now in avuncular form, invited us to the Hunt Ball, days out hunting, the point-to-point, and the rest. Life in North Wales seemed a world away from anything I had known before, and the roast lamb was delicious. However, when invited to have some more, we noticed the cats were up on the sideboard helping themselves to what was left of the joint. We decided we had had enough anyway!

Moving to Pen Parc was a leap in the dark. But we were young, and this was an adventure. The pull of the hills and vales, the extra fields we had acquired for the horses and ponies, the hunting on the doorstep, and the lifestyle, in complete contrast to our established existence, with many good friends and the familiarity of the Wirral, attracted me. I was following an intuition, a challenge, and this overrode any cautious thinking. In my mind there were echoes of the hunting stories and the thrilling *Mountain and Valley of Adventure* books by Enid Blyton, which I had read as a child. We had two young children of our own, but perhaps I hadn't grown up yet myself.

Pen Parc is a house of character in the Welsh long house style, and dates from the 17th century. The Welsh poet Twm O Nant was said to have dwelt there at that time, and the house is signed on most maps. Long houses were built of stone, and in those days they combined humans with livestock. The higher end of the house was occupied by people, while animals were tethered in the lower, allowing slurry to drain through the end wall. In later centuries long houses were enlarged, with an upper floor for bedrooms at the top end, and a hay loft for the animals at the lower. The ownership of an extensive long house was a sign of prosperity in the rural region, and they were occupied by landowning families, while the poorer tenants lived in more humble dwellings. Pen Parc is surrounded by hills, woods, streams and fields, and is tucked away in a valley with stunning views of the Clwydian range in the distance. The sound of bleating sheep, near and far, can be heard most of the time, with several small farms scattered nearby, and we soon became known to the Welsh farmers.

Before moving into Pen Parc the house required fumigation, so declared the local council inspectors. For two weeks all windows and doors were sealed, while potions and toxins were released into every nook and cranny, floorboards and roof. The lower end of the house was damp, and a damp course was set into the old brick and stone. A new oil-fuelled Aga, blue and shiny bright, replaced the ancient coke one. Two small, dark rooms became one large, light living area, and a wood-burning stove was installed. A jackdaw's nest was removed from the chimney of the open stone fireplace, which alleviated the smoke. The grey flaking paint on the outside of the house was scraped away, and the thick, uneven walls re-painted white.

The farmyard, from being awash with mud, was concreted, the barns and stables painted black and white, and the holes in the roofs, gaping up to the sky, were repaired. New stable doors arrived, and the potholes along the drive filled in. The council pest control department came to dispatch the rodent population in the outbuildings. Daphne once told me the story of rattus running round upstairs at Pen Parc one morning, being chased by dogs and children, and finally seeking refuge in the pocket of her dressing gown, with its whiskery head poking out of the top. Fortunately, when we moved in, they never ventured into the house.

Farm names were known by the addition of the names of the farmers who dwelt there. At the bottom of the hill was John Davis 'Pandy', who had eyed the car on my first visit to Henllan; up the hill on the left was Williams 'Cae Mawr', and Roberts 'Hafod' was further up on the right. The fields had names and at the back of the barns was 'maid's acre'. There was a story that some hundred years ago one of the maids from the house had been murdered in this field, hence the name. Pen Parc always had a friendly feel about it, and this story never bothered me. There were two acres of woodland with oak and other hardwood trees, and a stream meandered through the edge of the farmyard and along the hedge boundary. The traditional stone outbuildings consisted of an upper yard of cow byres, their heavy tie chains remaining, hay and grain stores, stables and a tack room, which housed the original sterilizing unit for the dairy herd. On the bottom yard were more stables converted from pigsties.

One winter evening, as I passed the tumble-down sty in the orchard, the silent white form of a barn owl swooped out of the low entrance, so close I could almost feel its ghostly wings brush my face. It is such a beautiful bird. With so many barn conversions their preferred homes are becoming scarce. I wish I had known then how privileged we were to have a barn owl living in our outbuilding. There was so much I was yet to learn about the countryside.

Barn Owl – such a beautiful bird

At the top of the drive stood a solid grey stone wall, with a wooden platform for collecting the milk churns. Turning left out of the drive took you steeply into the hills. Moel Fodiar rises up in the distance, a dark silhouette against the sky, and often topped with snow. To the left is Moel Twysog. These are high hill peaks with old springy turf interspersed with dense yellow gorse and purple heather. Rabbits popped in and out, their white scuts disappearing into the prickles as we cantered to the top – the wind pinching and whipping across our faces icy and sharp. The views from the summit of Moel Fodiar are spectacular. Climb to its height and gaze out towards the coast of Abergele, which spreads into the sparkling blue Irish Sea, and, turning inland, deep valleys sweep like vast mossy-green curtains dotted with creamy Welsh sheep. On a winter's day the same hills glower down, black and brooding amidst a sheet of pelting rain.

I never owned a pony as a child, but we always had dogs. Here in Wales we had three – later to be four. Sasha was a liver and white English pointer, and Millie a smooth-haired dachshund. When Kerry died, Zoe, a black spaniel, joined our family. Sasha and Millie went off hunting most days. They waited by the door and looked up at me hopefully, and then dashed off into the hills behind the house. Sasha bounded along like a lithesome deer, with Millie, a little reddish-brown figure, often taking the initiative and leading the way. They worked as a team. Sasha used her scenting instincts from the air while circling the covert, waiting for Millie to flush out a rabbit. She would also point, one front paw up, still and rigid with just a brown nose twitching, and Millie, with her short legs and nose to the ground, entered the undergrowth full of gusto, however thick and prickly. They stayed out for most of the morning, returning at lunch time, Sasha panting happily, eyes bright with the fun they had had, and Millie sporting bloody scratches on her nose. Dachshunds are real little hunters, and Millie was as game as any terrier. Twice I saw her catch a rat and dispatch it quick as a flash. Zoe was like all spaniels, very affectionate, and liked to be with me at home.

Large dogs do not live as long as small dogs, and Sasha, our beautiful, gentle dog was no different. Some years after we had moved to Wales, Tory was invited to take part in the prestigious Wylye Three-day Event in the Junior class. Sasha was about ten years old, and arthritic in her back legs. I decided to leave her behind in kennels on this occasion. How much I have regretted that decision. Wylye went well, and the Junior team selectors watched Tory with an eagle eye. We set off on the journey home from Wiltshire feeling buoyant, but our elation was short-lived.

Arriving at Pen Parc in the late afternoon, while we unloaded the trailer Christopher went to collect Sasha. Hearing the car returning down the drive, I looked up and saw Sasha sitting bolt upright on the back seat, tongue hanging out, literally smiling with pleasure to be home again. But it was her final effort. She had been ill at the kennels, and died that evening. She had hung on until she was at home with her family. I find this hard to write about even now. Losing one's dogs is always so painful. A friend of mine says her husband refuses to have another since their sheepdog died, unable to face the distress again. She added he had wept more than when his mother had gone, but actually I have heard that before from another friend, Simon Armstrong, when his Jack Russell died.

Sasha

While renovations took place and we were still living in Burton, we frequently loaded up two ponies into our wooden trailer and all four of us, as a family, piled into the Land-rover, and chugged our way to Pen Parc. Sasha and Zoe jumped into the back, while Millie was placed on the front seat, waiting to be hugged on someone's knee. Sometimes Jill, a lovely girl who used to babysit for us, came too with Dimple her donkey, and we somehow managed to squeeze him into the trailer too. A paraffin cooker, some sausages and soup, a plentiful supply of Mars bars completed the load, and off we went for the day.

This was the greatest of fun. The girls had the freedom of cantering round the newly acquired fields, making jumps out of logs and branches, troughs, and anything that looked jumpable, and scrambling or leaping over the stream. The ponies loved it and so did the dogs. Sheep were everywhere, grazing in neighbouring fields, but I had trained the dogs from a young age to leave well alone. It was February/March time and the empty house felt cold. However, we gathered round the little cooker and relished the hot soup and rather burnt sausages. Those were carefree, expectant days, and soon we would be hunting with the Flint and Denbigh hounds up in the hills behind our house, and in the valleys below.

THREE

HUNTING WITH THE FLINT AND DENBIGH HOUNDS – WE JOIN THE ASSOCIATED PONY CLUB

I was probably the typical very competitive Pony Club mother, the dread of all Pony Club DCs – District Commissioners. Certainly there was an occasion at a hunter trial when, somewhat exasperated, I left a truculent Polly behind in the unhitched trailer with her pony, while I took Tory to the dentist thirty minutes away, which meant she was on her own for about an hour and a half. Unfortunately a parent found her, and I think we were banned from competing for a while. But not for too long as, despite the ethos about competing for the fun of it, which of course is true, and not just to win, it also became apparent that the Lyon girls regularly produced good results, and therefore pride to their relevant branch. Achieving a balance is the aim, but not always easy at the time.

We soon joined the Flint and Denbigh Hunt branch of the Pony Club, which was founded in 1946 by the Hon. Mrs. Hotham and Mrs. Anne Clegg. Meg Hotham was a member of the Williams-Wynn family and, along with serving as District Commissioner of this branch of the Pony Club, she was joint master of the Flint and Denbigh foxhounds. She was of the old school, and would borrow ponies for children who did not have their own and persuade instructors to teach them, for free.

Minding your Ps and Qs, and knowing the unwritten rules when out hunting, was quite important to avoid an embarrassing reprimand from the Master of the day, in front of the whole field. The cardinal sin of all sins was if your horse kicked a hound. Kicking another horse was extremely unpopular, but not altogether unknown in a crowded gateway, and a human was bad enough, but a hound – oh dear me no! This could mean a public hanging, or at the very least sending home immediately, whoever you were. I recall a delightful lady, tall and of statuesque bearing, who was well known on the hunting field. Her name was Marigold, and her horse committed the unmentionable and kicked a hound in a narrow lane. A terrible howling and yelping ensued, and everyone stood up in their stirrups to see what had happened. There followed a torrent of furious and fruity language at the guilty steed, and the lady then cantered off home, flame-coloured curls bobbing crossly through the hair net beneath her bowler hat.

My early experience of hunting with the Flint and Denbigh, or the 'funk and dawdle' as it was sometimes known, (but as we neither funked, nor dawdled when it mattered, I never called them the latter name) was on a dark bay ex-racehorse named Metrilla. She was a good jumper but it had to be at racing pace. Having sighted a fence, she exploded. Up, over and away. She could also be a handful. There was plenty of galloping country in The Vale but there were some steep banks around a thickly-wooded area called Bont Newydd – New Bridge. Hounds were running, and we were attempting to leave the woods. The path was narrow and heavily overhung with trees. One horse tucked in behind the other, bumping along at a choppy canter, we crouched low over the saddle, ducking and diving to avoid being smacked in the face by branches. Metrilla had been a racehorse and she objected to being behind. She plunged and bucketed along the path, nose in her chest. The person in front on a sensible cob kept turning round in fear of being leapt on, and I just smiled at her through clenched teeth.

We entered a clearing and fanned out. Ahead was Willy Tilley, field master that day.

'Hold hard,' he shouted back, 'it's the butter slide.'

Now some riders clearly knew this place, and gathered up the reins. I had never been there before. With a rampaging Metrilla, swathes of foamy white sweat dripping down her neck, I found myself at the lip of a drop of about twenty feet of packed wet mud. To the left and to the right, the more sensible horses and native ponies were slipping and sliding sideways, or picking their way, heads down, looking where they were going. Not so Metrilla; hovering at the top, she launched herself like Eddie the Eagle, all four feet in the air, with me hanging on for dear life.

Landing half way down, and before she could repeat the performance, I bailed out, and leapt from the saddle. Throwing the reins at her, I hoped someone would catch her for me at the bottom. Fortunately hunting people are mostly chivalrous, and a gentleman grabbed Metrilla's reins as she plunged down. Legging me quickly back into the saddle, he said, laughing, 'Did you mean to do that?' 'Oh yes,' I said, 'it seemed the safer option,' and jamming down my bowler hat, off we galloped to the sound of speaking hounds.

Living at Pen Parc, our lives took on a pattern. In the winter we hunted, and in the summer we competed with the ponies. I cannot think of a time in my life when I have enjoyed myself more. Lawn meets on Saturdays were convivial, social occasions, and mostly held in the best galloping and jumping part of the country. Followers on foot gathered round on the lawns of fine houses, and mounted followers collected on gravel forecourts or in the fields adjacent. We were treated to glasses of port, sausage rolls and fruit cake. Favourite venues were Plas Heaton, Greenfields, and Gyrn Castle. Gyrn Castle was the castellated mansion home of Sir Geoffrey Bates, whose family had originated from a successful shipping company in Liverpool. Geoffrey, awarded an MC during the war, was a brave follower of hounds on his steadfast hunter, Sam. Together they completed the Hunt race at the Flint and Denbigh point-to-point, along with Mike Sheridan on a heavyweight hunter. Probably finishing a circuit behind the rest of the field, they were greeted with a great cheer and raised glasses from hunt supporters as they jumped the last fence.

Friends and fellow enthusiasts arrived mounted on an assortment of horses and ponies. There were scarlet coats, black and navy jackets, tweed for children and sometimes for farmers. Top hats, bowlers and peaked velvet caps (no one wore crash hats in those days). This all presented a colourful picture, along with well turned out thoroughbreds and quality hunters, fully clipped and plaited. Jill Smith's former Wembley show hunter, Bunowen, was a classic example of the latter. However, he was rather precious, and usually went home early! Michael Griffith, sometime acting field master, liked a thoroughbred horse, and was always one to follow when hounds were running. Joint Master Richard Heaton was never in a hurry, and had a penchant for singing nursery rhymes as he cantered sedately along – perhaps not one to follow when hounds were running.

The Tilley family turned up in force. Willy, unmistakable aboard the heavyweight hunter The Guv'nor. Four children mounted; Tuffy with Tom Temp, her future British team member, John on Topic, a sharp thoroughbred and one of a twin, just 14.3hh. David rode Marmite, a glossy brown pony who had a talent for dropping his shoulder and depositing his jockey in the mud, but seldom David, who knew him too well. Lavinia rode the trusty chestnut cob, Colonel. Colonel was ageless. He was as slow as a boat, but like the tortoise he always arrived eventually. Daphne followed by car with flasks of tea for anyone in need, and Dicka preferred his bike. There were reliable Irish hunters and horses of indiscriminate breeding, smartly turned out ponies like Pippa and Kim Smith's and tough little hairy ponies. The Brookes family from Ystrad Farm supported en masse; five girls, Mary, Sandy, who went well at Badminton with Welton Playboy, Janet, Helen and Rachel, and of course mother Joan. Helen was soon to be chatted up by chicken farmer Ricki Proffitt, and became Mrs. Proffitt, and Ricki eventually took over joint mastership of the F and D. Father, George Brookes, still sprightly, we often see at Bangor races.

We gave our ponies a blanket clip – which basically means clipping head, neck, shoulders and belly, and leaving where a rug would go, unclipped. I made sure Tory and Polly were well turned out, and the day before was spent kneeling on the floor surrounded by tack. Boots, bits and stirrups were polished to a sparkle, and leather was rubbed with Neatsfoot oil. For the next day's hunting, in their jacket pockets they each had a sandwich, a packet of fruit gums, with instructions to remember to share them with anyone standing nearby, a Kit-Kat, and their 'cap' – money for the day.

Soon I abandoned hunting Metrilla; the excitement was getting too much. But I was lent a particularly nice liver chestnut thoroughbred x Welsh Cob section C, called Nantcol Topbird. I really enjoyed the two seasons I hunted her. She stood still at the coverts, never pulled or lagged behind, was reliable over a fence, scopey enough for the bigger hedges, and clever jumping out of bog and over trappy rails. Tory's first hunting pony was Crispy. She was ten years old and the little palomino pony, by the stallion, Potato, that we had acquired from the Catherston stud, was as keen as mustard. They had some wonderful days hunting together. We sold Crispy to future eventing International, Polly Clarke, now Stockton, and he continued his hunting with the Wynstay hounds.

Soon a Welsh Mountain pony of the old fashioned section B type, a flying white Pegasus called Lydstep Rudolph, joined our growing equine population. Although officially grey, Rudolph was snowy white and came from a local farming family, Mr. and Mrs. Ken Owen, who also trained point-to-pointers; he had been outgrown by their son

Mark, was in his teens, and had not been ridden for over a year. I paid £200 for him and bought him untried, unvetted and straight from the field. Rudolph was a 14.1hh pony variety of Desert Orchid, the legendary grey steeplechaser, with the same get up and go, hang on to your hats attitude. Brilliant over a fence, he became well known at all the Pony Club events from the Albrighton in Worcestershire to the Wynstay in Cheshire, the Tanatside in Shropshire and the West Lancs up in the north, taking both Tory and Polly to the championships four times. However, to begin with he presented us with tough challenges. Rudolph had been sent to Scotland on trial for a competitive family. He was promptly returned as unrideable. We were soon to find out why.

Horses are perceptive, and if Rudolph felt his rider was unsure, he would simply grab the bit and run away. Round and round the field he would go, white tail streaming out behind like the wake from a jet in the sky. Ten times round the show ring with judge in the middle scratching his head. Headlong towards the gate, Rudolph thundered on, while his jockey stuck her feet in the stirrups and hauled on the reins like Boadicea in a war chariot. Rudolph was a pony, but he thought he was a racehorse. Of course he did. He was used to training alongside the Owens' point-to-pointers, and that is what he did, gallop as fast as he could to keep up.

There was only one thing to do. I decided to hunt him myself for a season, and hoped for a solution with time. This by and large worked. Rudolph was an exciting ride, to say the least, but I never doubted him, and he jumped hedges, ditches, gates and forded rivers, the water lapping over my boots as we half swam, half strode through a surging torrent of River Elwy flood. Typical pony, he enjoyed sharing my lunch, and with a break at a covert side, and horses blowing and pawing at the ground, steam rising from them like a frothy cloud in the brisk winter air, Rudolph turned his head as I put my hand in my pocket and whickered through quivering nostrils.

The best hunts are often to be had towards the end of the day. The field has thinned and the intrepid are still out. We rarely came home early, not wanting to miss that final thrill of a late run. If I hoped for a steady reflective return to the parked horse box, possibly drenched with stiff freezing fingers, no such luck. Rudolph insisted on throwing his head up and down, up and down, refused to walk, and jiggled and joggled all the way in the fading light, at which point, with the saddle by now resembling a plank of wood, I couldn't wait to get off him. Once home, there was no groom to hand him over to. It was set to, wash him off, keep him warm, check for cuts, and make him comfortable in his stable with a well-earned feed. Only then was it inside to the warm house, pull off the muddy boots, throw down the wet jacket and sodden gloves, and leave the sweaty tack till tomorrow.

We were riding in the fields when we heard yelping from the lane at the top of our drive. The tone was desperate and pitiful. I sent the children on ponies to investigate. They returned cradling a small black and white puppy, with a pink nose dotted with black markings. It could not have been more than six or seven weeks old. It wriggled in their arms, whining. I quickly produced a bowl of milk. I have never seen an animal so hungry and went to fetch another. We called the puppy Hedgerow, so named by us because that is where she had been abandoned, tucked away at the bottom of the hedge. I rang our dog vet in Denbigh, Trevor Pritchard, who said she was one of four left around the area. We happily kept her and she grew to be a medium-sized lovely dog.

So with Sasha, Zoe and Millie, our canine population had now stretched to four. Perhaps word had got around in the local animal kingdom to head for Pen Parc, because before long two cats arrived from where we know not, and on separate occasions. Rubbing themselves up at the kitchen window pane outside, they mewed hopefully and persistently. Edward was a large tabby cat that gazed at you with appealing green eyes like shiny, speckled marbles, and Sarah was a beautifully-marked tortoiseshell with a snowy white chest. Of course I gave them some milk and they stayed with us and lived outside in the barns.

We had a young horse called Secret Venture, stable name Charlie. He was a bright bay by Paper Cap, a popular stallion standing in Shropshire. Secret Venture had cracked a bone and spent several months in his stable, recovering. Some horses tolerate dogs and cats coming in and out of their stables, and others flatten their ears and strike out with their forelegs, making it quite clear that other animals are not welcome in their 'houses'. Charlie was the latter and showed it in no uncertain terms. Edward liked the horses. I often saw him rubbing his head up and down their legs in the stables. He soon struck up an empathy with Charlie during those tedious months. Edward loved to be picked up, pushing his furry striped face against your cheek, purring deeply like a rumbling bear. I noticed he would jump into Charlie's stable or slide in by my legs when I opened the door. To begin with I shooed him out; I did not want a battered feline lying in the straw. But Edward persisted, appearing as the day drew to a close, after the last feed, and the stable yard became quiet. There was a beam in the corner of Charlie's stable and the horse would place himself near, and wait for Edward to jump lightly onto it, balancing on his velvety paws, while Charlie closed his eyes as the cat rubbed his head against the horse's face. I instinctively knew that Charlie would not hurt him. Animals have extraordinary powers of perception. This story reminds me of another involving an adored little tan terrier I had, called Sparkle, which will come later.

There is nothing like hunting to teach children stickability and perseverance. It is extremely inconvenient to fall off. Out hunting one Boxing Day, with Tory and Crispy well ahead of the field, I stayed near the back with Rudolph. This was out of character, but I had a responsibility. With me was an eight year old Polly on a small pony called Specky, borrowed from the Tilleys. The pony knew his job well.

'Follow me, Polly,' I shouted, as we approached a decent hedge.

She did so in spectacular style. Turning round I saw the pair of them flying through the air – but they weren't together. There were a few foot followers standing by the said hedge.

'Oh, the poor little thing,' cried a lady, rushing to scoop up Polly.

With a stomping Rudolph snatching at his bridle, the reaction from her mother was a bit different.

'Quickly, put her back in the plate, hounds are running, we mustn't lose them – come on, Polly!'

Hunting teaches children the ways of the countryside, and good manners. You have to consider the farmer, and keep to the edge of his fields if they are sown or very wet, and to say thank you if you clatter through his farmyard. You must always shut gates. One hunting day we were trotting across a field to draw another covert, when Willy called back to Vinny. 'Lavinia, dismount and disentangle that sheep caught in wire – look sharp about it.'

It is automatic to say good morning to the Master, and good night is customary, whatever the time of day when deciding to go home. The hounds are valuable creatures and children learn to turn their ponies' heads towards them if they pass in a narrow lane. The F and D were good at encouraging the next generation and the girls were often given jobs to do, perhaps holding a whip's horse, opening gates and sometimes put 'on point'. There was a ritual when returning from hunting. It was usually after 4pm and daylight was fading. Both ponies would be splattered with mud from their ears to their stifles, thrown up from large hunters galloping ahead of them. With one grey and the other palomino, and having arrived at the meet spotless, hooves oiled, tails brushed, and tack supple and shining, it was a very different image at the end of the day.

We had an old cast iron bath in the downstairs cloakroom at Pen Parc, and with two bridles caked in earth, there was only one thing to do; I dumped them, along with stirrups, girths and leathers, into the bath and ran the taps. They did, of course, need saddle soap afterwards, but that at least removed the worst. The ponies were made comfortable in deep straw-bedded stables. We thatched them and loosely bandaged their legs over straw, and brushed them off the next day when dry. Bundles of straw were stuffed under jute rugs and made secure. This is quite old-fashioned but it kept them warm and they never broke out in a sweat. They were given a bran mash and later their usual mix of pony nuts and sugar beet or barley.

We had no help with our horses and ponies, and both girls and I were responsible for complete care of them. This was hard work, especially when the weather was freezing with ice and snow, but caring for all our animals I found pleasurable and satisfying. One of Daphne Tilley's remedies for a clipped horse with a sore back was to dab on spirit. Willy's hunter, The Guv'nor, was always given whisky after a hard day's hunting – it would be spread in liberal doses along his back.

Horse rugs forty years ago were usually made of jute, often with a grey wool lining. When the weather turned very cold, clipped horses had extra blankets which were put underneath, folded back across the withers, and all kept in place with an over girth or surcingle. Cotton sheets were used as an initial layer. With the passing of winter Daphne decided to give her horse blankets a spring clean at the local launderette in Denbigh. The machines were bigger than domestic ones at home, and took two or three blankets at once. Launderettes were quite sociable places – you could even get an automated plastic mug of tea or coffee whilst waiting. Several machines stood in rows whirring and tumbling away, and opposite them were benches where you sat inanely, watching what other people had in their wash, or struck up a conversation with the person sitting next to you. I will recall Daphne's version of events.

'I had finished one load of blankets,' she told me, 'when a woman came in and put a pile of nappies (terry towelling in those days) into the machine I had just emptied. With her wash completed, and as I bundled together my second lot, I noticed the woman staring, aghast, at her "clean" nappies. They were all covered in chestnut hairs, sticking out of the nappies like a porcupine.'

A few days later a notice was put up in the launderette. 'Horse blankets must not be used in these machines.'

There was something very rewarding after a long energetic day out hunting, frequently in wet and cold weather, galloping across hills and vales, with the challenge of jumping anything that came your way, then returning home and making sure the horses and ponies were warm and comfortable in their stables – tucking them up as it were; and finally, when the work was done, going indoors to a cheery fire, tea and crumpets and the hysterical Basil Brush show on television. This was followed by the menacing tones of Doctor Who. Basil Brush was a fox; a ginger-coloured glove puppet with buck teeth and a braying laugh. 'Boom boom!' he shouted, with a nudge, nudge and a far back voice. 'It's a brush, not a tail, don't ye know.'

It took me some years to appreciate the unconventional ways of the Tilley family but, looking back, what I initially learnt about hunting, and later eventing, was rooted in our participation with the Flint and Denbigh hounds, the associated Pony Club and the Tilleys. As time went on, I learnt from other people too, notably British International and former European champion Rachel Bayliss. Despite my time at the Wirral Riding Centre, my non-horsey background meant I had to learn the hard way and make mistakes. I took risks, some regrettable, and relied on gut instinct, a determination to succeed and a certain 'eye for a horse'. It is unlikely that much of the contents in the following chapters could be written without the experience of those early action-packed days in North Wales. There was also something I was scarcely conscious of at first – a desire to excel, and in something that I loved and took a serious interest in. Almost without awareness, my mother's words touched a chord in my mind.

'Always aspire to do your best,' she would say in a strong voice.

I never rode competitively myself, but I was lucky; I had two daughters who did.

The Pony Club Championships were held every year at Stoneleigh Park in Warwickshire. Qualifying for this was the aim of competitive members from all over the country, from Scotland to Cornwall and across to Northern Ireland. Lydstep Rudolph was our Flint and Denbigh team pony member with Tory and Polly, along with, at various times, James Griffith, Tuffy and John Tilley, Rachel Brookes, Jane Duscherer, Kimberley Ellery, Biddig Lloyd and Fenella Fawcus. The Cheshire teams were hot competition and difficult to beat. Smart and expensive animals, particularly in the Cheshire North branch, were not uncommon. From the Cheshire teams the main contenders were Caroline Scott, Linda Budenberg, Katy Weston, Jason Varey, Simon Ashworth, Zoe Hancox, Miranda Parton, Beverley Ridge and others. Vera Holden instructed several people in Cheshire. She was, of course, a protégé of the renowned trainer Eddie Goldman.

Provided you could steer, Rudolph was outstanding, and it never occurred to him to refuse; he loved jumping and had the innate pony intelligence of taking care of himself, and consequently his jockey. Covering the ground in an easy gallop with a sense of purpose, his ears twitched backwards and forwards as he measured his stride before a jump. Watching Red Rum I noticed he did this, too. A horse with great intelligence, he knew how huge the National fences were, and he was not a flamboyant jumper, but as clever and nimble as a cat, with a great sense of self preservation.

I am convinced Rudolph looked for the red and white flags flanking the jumps as he travelled across the country. He liked to be in charge and took a good hold, and you did need spunk to ride him, but if you had confidence in him he never let you down. However, if he caught you not concentrating, or dithering without an encouraging leg on his sides, he could, on rare occasions, jink out, and this happened twice, both at the championships, the first with Tory. She had a stop at the water fence and fazed by this, she then lost her way. Waiting near the finish in my usual state of agitation, I peered into the distance, trying to spot our dashing white pony, when I heard the commentator.

'Victoria Lyon from the Flint and Denbigh seems to be taking the scenic route, and is presently heading off towards a field of stubble, and the main road.' The pair found their way back on course, but picked up several time faults.

The second time was with Polly. With a leading dressage score, a win was on the cards, and she set off, perhaps defensively, and had a run out also at the water. Completing the course, Rudolph galloped through the finish with a thunderous Polly. Collapsing onto the pony's neck, she exclaimed in anguish, 'I'm *useless*, utterly useless!'

I met Rachel Bayliss at a lecture demonstration held at the Brookes' farm near Denbigh. We subsequently held several training clinics at Pen Parc for keen eventers from Cheshire and North Wales. Rachel came as trainer and arrived with two Weimaraner dogs. Rachel and the dogs stayed with us in the house while riders camped in their horse boxes. These clinics were educational and fun. Along with the serious training there was a party atmosphere. A great stalwart of those days was Hazel Ridge. Hazel was the work horse who willingly rolled up her sleeves on the domestic front, cooking, washing up, tidying, chivvying and so on, while the rest of us were immersed with the horses. Every year, Hazel gathers us up for a Pony Club reunion lunch. From the age of thirteen Polly spent many months training with Rachel at her base at Somerford Park, Cheshire. Rachel is a top-rate trainer and had a lasting influence on Polly's early eventing career. Somerford Park is now an International training centre, with acres of cross-country fences and impeccable schooling arenas.

With an expanding animal population, preparing for the Boxing Day meet, while enjoying Christmas Day too, needed planning. The Boxing Day meet was the highlight of the Christmas week. I recall the gloom one year when the hounds had kennel cough and hunting was abandoned. Pen Parc lent itself to Christmas; the house exuded atmosphere. With the beams and low ceilings, thick stone walls, the open fire and the permanent heat of the Aga, it was a welcome and cheery place. The Hunt Supporters club and the Pony Club organised carol singing, and we lit candles as they gathered in the kitchen and sang familiar carols. Drinks and mince pies followed and it set the tone for the festivities to come. Christmas Eve included Midnight Mass at St. Bueno's in Tremeirchion. Built in 1848, St. Bueno's is a monastery. A large and imposing grey stone building set high in the hills, it is the residence of an order of Jesuit monks.

The 19th century poet, Gerard Manley Hopkins, wrote many of his greatest poems whilst residing at St Bueno's. From the college he looked across the valley of the Elwy and to the Welsh mountains and wrote:

Lovely the woods, waters, meadows, coombes, vales
All the air things wear that build this world of Wales.

A few years ahead of Tory and Polly, Tuffy Tilley had been taking part in Junior and Young Rider eventing team trials, and was soon talent spotted by the British selectors. I watched her progress from Pony Club to team selection. I had been absorbing knowledge during our years in North Wales. I was always looking for the best trainers, the best vets and the best farriers. Richard Owen was our horse vet in North Wales. Son of trainer Hollister Owen, Richard came from an equine background, and had the natural instinct of a horseman. 'That's not a tendon,' he reassured us, feeling a horse's rather puffy leg after a day's hunting. 'There is probably a little thorn in there, somewhere.'

Sure enough, he was right. John Hughes was the best farrier within miles, and every month I boxed up two, occasionally three, horses to his smithy in Malpas, Cheshire. John never travelled. The trip was an arduous whole day away, but I am obsessive about horses' feet, and this kept my mind reassured.

As I observed and learnt, I became familiar with the formalities of team trials, long lists and short lists, selection committees, and the training scholarships funded by animal feed merchants, Spillers, held at Gill Watson's training establishment at Aston Rowant in Buckinghamshire. A Fellow of the British Horse Society, Gill was the Junior and Young Rider British team trainer. The Junior National Eventing Championships at Windsor became a distant target, and I began to weigh up possible trials, and search for suitable horses. I also ignored the rumour that if you lived north of Birmingham your chances of making the team were minimal.

FOUR

WINDSOR – TUSSLER – THE
COLONELS – SPONSORSHIP

The British Junior National Championships were held annually at Windsor Great Park, by courtesy of Her Majesty the Queen. Competing at Windsor was a privilege given to around twenty-five Juniors selected from the various trials around the country. This unique venue retained a prestige which elevated competing there to a level of the very best. The avenue of trees – the Long Walk, which is over two miles long, and disappears into the distance as you gaze down from the top of the hill, beneath the magnificent copper statue of King George III – was an inspiration, and receiving an invitation to compete at Windsor was hugely exciting.

One year, Tory and I chugged up the M6 in our ancient wooden horse box to the historic site of Brougham Castle, on the River Eamont in Cumbria, for our first official horse trial. We were put up in a turreted manor house, owned by two middle-aged bachelor brothers. It was March and, typically of many old country estates, the house was freezing. The next morning we woke to a white landscape, as snow had fallen during the night. Outside we fed the horse in his stable and then, back in the house to the smell of grilling bacon, we made our way to the dining room for breakfast on a large white-clothed table. We helped ourselves to the selection on the oval, covered silver platters laid out on the sideboard. One brother was cooking on a blackened range in the kitchen, and the other poured our coffee. It was quite bizarre, but they were extremely hospitable. Upstairs we discovered Millie curled up in the suitcase amongst our clothes, making sure she would not be left behind in the cold house. The snow cleared, Tory won her section and was immediately invited to Windsor by talent spotter and team selector, Mrs Audrey Locket. It was a proud moment, but we declined that year, as her horse was inexperienced. In 1983 she was again invited to compete at the championships, where she did well on a horse called Tussler.

Tussler came from a dealer in the Midlands. He was an attractive chestnut horse and he was also cheap. I have only once paid a ridiculous price for a horse. It was a moment of stupidity, and this horse did not reach the expectations he promised. I find it a challenge to find horses for a snip and make something of them. Tussler was aptly named because we were to have many, many tussles with Tussler. The dealer's son jumped on his back, and I noticed he gave Tussler a couple of digs in the ribs with a pair of very long spurs. Maybe I should have heeded that warning sign, but I liked the horse, a deal was made, and Tussler duly arrived at Pen Parc.

The strict regulations that apply today when buying and selling horses, regarding stable vices, were not adhered to in the same way thirty or forty years ago. Nor did vets routinely lunge horses on a hard surface, or take blood samples for evidence of drugs when vetting them for purchase. Rather than a fail or a pass as previously, vets today can recommend a horse or not, for the purpose for which it is being purchased. This can give a much broader analysis and rather puts the onus on the purchaser, which I think is probably quite sensible, as price can often be negotiated in the case of what is known as an 'if'.

We soon discovered that Tussler was a weaver, which is classified as a stable vice. A weaver is a horse who waves his head from side to side over the stable door, either spasmodically or chronically. If the latter, they can lose condition. A horse with a nap is one who has learnt evasive action to going the way you ask them, which is 99.5 percent of the time forwards. You see it sometimes on the racecourse, when a horse refuses to start. Tussler had a 'nappy' streak in his character, hence the long spurs on first viewing. One day we took him to a show, along with a pony. The pony class was first, and Tussler was left by himself in the trailer. Returning to the horse box park I saw our trailer rocking violently, much akin to a gyrating Elvis Presley belting out Jailhouse Rock with as much noise; a crashing and banging as Tussler threw himself from side to side like a horse demented. Pony and I ran as fast as we could and, soaked in sweat, flanks heaving, Tussler soon calmed down. Once settled in his new home, he stopped weaving, except at feed times. But Tussler did well, and Tory won with him in a hot contest at Weston Park; we then decided he had reached his limit with us, and we sold him to a family where he won his section at the Pony Club Championships. I was pleased as, despite his problems, I had a soft spot for the horse.

However, one day I would willingly have sent him to the Hunt kennels. Polly was thirteen and had occasionally ridden Tussler, but only when I was around. She wanted to hack him out by herself and my answer was an emphatic 'No.' After relentless pushing, and against my better judgement, I caved in. Watching them disappear up the drive I checked my watch. If they were not back within forty minutes I would be out in the car searching. About twenty-five minutes had passed, when something made me glance up at the window. A chestnut banshee, a vision of panic, was heading full pelt down the drive, clouds of dust and gravel spitting out behind. Tussler, nostrils flaring, reins by his knees, stirrups flying and riderless.

Rushing out of the back door, I met him clattering into the stable yard. Hurling him into a stable still tacked up, and throwing the door shut, I leapt into the car and sped towards Cefn Berain about a mile away. As I reached the crest of the hill I could make out something lying in the road. I knew it would be Polly and it was. The emotions that went through my head in those few seconds are indescribable. She was OK, but very sore. Having got her safely into hospital, I did not ask for explanations. I guessed Tussler had wanted to go one way and Polly another, so Tussler had reverted to his naughty tricks, and deposited his jockey on the ground.

In the 1980s the Junior selection panel were smilingly labelled 'the Colonels'. There were three of them. These were Colonel Hubert Allfrey MC, Colonel Henry Nicoll DSO, and Colonel Bill Lithgow. They overlapped each other at different times, and it was universally understood that, while the most important thing was for the British Juniors to come home with gold medals, the worst scenario of all was to be beaten by the Germans, who were usually our nearest rivals. The Colonels saw the European championships as an extension of the war! There is an historical slant to this, as the sport of eventing evolved from the use of horses in battle. A fit, courageous and well-trained horse was vital in order to survive. The three phases of eventing are akin to the attributes required in a war horse. No better description of these is given than in the book *Warrior* by General Jack Seeley, grandfather of racing journalist, Brough Scott, who pens the introduction. There is that other great story of a war horse in the riveting stage show of the same name.

Dressage is demonstrated in the discipline of good training, the speed and endurance, or cross-country, in the fitness and courage to gallop over any obstacle or terrain for many miles, and finally showjumping, to prove that despite the rigours of the previous day, your horse is willing and able to carry on. On the continent, the sport of eventing was known as the Military, and two posters I still have from three-day-events in Zonhoven, Belgium, and Boekelo in Holland, have the heading 'Military' across the top.

In 1987, during the Junior European Championships in the impressive setting of the Centro Equestre Federale at Pratoni del Vivaro, south of the eternal city of Rome, Germany and Great Britain were neck and neck, with their top placed competitors the final two to show-jump. The Colonels were watching keenly and grimly. Was it to be a German or British flag that was slowly raised to the top of the white pole that year, and would disaster for the Colonels prevail or be averted by the hand of fate? All will be revealed.

'I don't want to be labelled a pushy mother,' I said to chairman of Junior selectors, Hubert Allfrey, one day.

'Hmmph!' he grunted, steely eyes peering under bushy eyebrows, military moustache twitching.

'It depends how you push and whether you have a rider worth pushing.'

Hubert Allfrey had a somewhat gruff manner and he could look quite fierce, but he was also kind, and as time went on and both Tory and Polly showed distinct promise, he did everything he could to encourage us and, along with other prospective team members and parents, we were invited to his comfortable house in Shipton Moyne, Gloucestershire, for dinner. These were convivial evenings and we always had an excellent meal, cooked by his housekeeper. However, some of the chairs, brought in from the garden, were rather low, and if you ended up on one of these you found yourself with your knife and fork somewhere near your ears, resembling a begging dog, trying to negotiate the food on your plate, while Hubert sat at the head, staring gleefully down at us through his glinting spectacles. He was very proud of his Junior teams, and in his dining room on the wall above his fish aquarium, he had photographs of them all through the years.

Before that longed-for invitation to Windsor was given, all potential candidates were scrutinised during the early trials and competitions. Polly, aged seventeen, was competing at Henbury Hall in Cheshire when she was hauled up in front of the stewards for over-use of the whip. Sometimes horses need a smack; like children, they can be disobedient, and will test your authority. They are big, powerful creatures and an unruly horse is a dangerous one. Polly was riding a horse called Weasel; he was a smart, rich bay, purchased from Carmen Lanni, with a white blaze down his face and two white socks. She was carrying a whip with a flappy bit of leather on the end. It made a lot of noise but barely touched the horse. As they approached fence three on the cross-country, Weasel put on the brakes and danced determinedly sideways on his hind legs, with another fifteen obstacles ahead to be tackled.

Thwack, thwack, whappity whap whap, slapitty slap slap. A noise like a pistol shot whistled through the air in rapid succession, originating from around Weasel's backside.

With a leap skywards, Weasel changed his mind and bounded over the fence. The pair then galloped off, grass flying, with Polly hunched over the saddle like Piggott in a finish, and another thwack, thwack, slappity slap to make sure. Meanwhile the jump judge was feverishly scribbling down her number and reporting back to base through her walkie-talkie. We thought the incident could be kept under wraps, but we discovered that Colonel Nicoll happened to be at Henbury that day. Henry Nicoll was an approachable and friendly man, but he was on the Junior selection panel and Polly was summoned. Eventually she reappeared, smiling. 'Oh, he just patted me on the shoulder and said, "Be careful next time you use your whip, Polly, but off you go. I know some horses can be a bit nappy."'

Sponsorship in eventing was a popular topic at that time. Lucinda Prior-Palmer, later Green, was probably the first to ride under a company sponsorship. We were at the annual Grand National party in Thurstaston on the Wirral, hosted by our chums Kit and Janie Jackson. At the party was Christopher Banner, who owned companies with the oil and chemical industries. He had been a guest of ICI in the hospitality marquee at the British National Championships at Gatcombe Park, and was clearly impressed with the experience. Home of HRH the Princess Royal, Gatcombe Park in Gloucestershire attracts thousands of spectators, plus the cream of competitors, and the setting is second to none, with magnificent viewing.

I had known Christopher for many years; I knew he liked a challenge. I took a punt. 'Polly could be competing at Gatcombe next year,' I said.

This was unlikely, but I had ignited an interest.

'I will support her, ring me in the morning,' said Christopher.

Next morning I rang the number of Samuel Banner and Co. Ltd. in Liverpool, and true to his word Christopher came up with an initial sponsorship for two years. This was later to stretch to five. It was a huge boost, both financially and to our morale, and his generosity and enthusiasm will always be appreciated.

This was not the only wager I had that day. Our friend Denis Coltart had a share in a racehorse, so we were soon discussing the highs and lows of horse ownership.

'My horse had a win the other day,' said Denis.

'Oh, that's brilliant,' said I, and not to be outdone replied, 'Polly is riding at Windsor in May.'

'Is she any good?' said Denis.

'Well, I expect she will ride in a British team one day.'

'I'll have a tenner with you that she won't,' said Denis, grinning.

'Done,' I said, and stuck my hand out.

Two years later, I won my tenner, because I had already seen an advertisement in *Horse and Hound* for a horse with a golden dun colour and black-tipped ears. His name was Highland Road.

FIVE

HIGHLAND ROAD

Under an ash tree, in the corner of a Wiltshire garden, is a grassy mound. It is a noticeable mound because beneath lies a horse. As spring arrives, crocuses push up through the grass – bright dots of colour – purple, white and yellow. Children ride ponies nearby, and call to each other across the paddock. Tractors drone in the distance, and Jack Russell terriers growl and snuffle under the hedges; they dig with ferocious paws, and mud flies in all directions. Hares may dash zigzag fashion in the fields adjacent and roe deer, easily alarmed, bounce quickly away through the grass. In the gloom of dusk a fox can be spotted trotting past, brush low to the ground. We are in Wilton Pony Club and Hunt country, and the family hunters gaze over the post and rail fence. They nudge and push each other in the pecking order as horses do, and wait to be lead down the pebbly track to their stables, and evening feed.

Hares may dash zigzag fashion

The horse lying peacefully in this garden was called Highland Road. A hint of Scotland, you may say, and you would be right. Highland Road was born on a farm in Worcestershire, but his story began far away on the island of Rum in the Hebrides – an island of mist-shrouded mountains rising craggy from a remote landscape. A very different scene to the grassy plains around Salisbury where he spent his final years.

On Rum today there is a herd of ponies. They are lighter and smaller than the Highland pony from the mainland, and stand no more than 13.2 hands high. They come in many colours, including black, grey, chestnut and dun. Some have unusual flaxen or silvery manes and tails, as well as the more familiar black. In 1775 the Laird of Rum described them as small and beautiful. Many of the ponies are semi-feral, and others are used to carry deer down from the hills during the cull. They may have existed on the island since the Ice Age. Rum is one of Britain's largest wild life reserves, and along with the ponies there are seals, otters, golden eagles, feral goats and red deer. Travelling to the island by ferry from Malaig, you must leave your car behind, as only cars belonging to the few residents are permitted.

Now imagine a picture a long time ago. It is 1934 and a herd of Highland ponies stand motionless against a backdrop of violet heather hills, their long sweeping manes and tails blowing in the sharp mountain breeze. They stare with caution at a young woman watching them; she was on her honeymoon in Scotland, and she loved horses. She noted that many were a golden dun colour with a black dorsal stripe running from wither to dock. Curiously their forelegs were marked with zebra-like stripes, seen on the original wild horse thousands of years ago. Turning to her new husband she said wistfully, 'I wish I could own one of those beautiful ponies.'

Fifty years later, in 1984, there was an obituary in *Horse and Hound* about a lady called Dorothy MacKenzie. This is an excerpt:

The death of Dorothy MacKenzie leaves a gap in the wide circle of friendship that her love of horses created. Born at about the turn of the century, the breeding of horses and Jack Russell terriers captured her imagination. Starting with a Highland pony mare, purchased on the Isle of Rum...

This lady was the one on her honeymoon in 1934, and as you will see some wishes really do come true.

It was 1939 and the threat of WW2 loomed, when a little Highland pony, bright golden dun in colour, peered from the door of a train carriage; she blinked as she stepped from the darkness on to a station platform. Waiting to greet her was Dorothy Mackenzie. The pony, born far away on the remote island of Rum, had sailed across the sea, and trundled her way to Umberleigh in Devon. Dorothy broke her pony to harness and rode her, too. People wanted to do their bit for the war effort, and with her pony and trap Dorothy travelled the Devon lanes, collecting anything that could be recycled from the farms around. When the war ended the pony, named Rum, after her birthplace, was sent to a thoroughbred stallion bred by Lord Derby, called Legendary.

Spring arrived, and Rum produced a dun filly foal. This filly was the dam of thirteen foals, all by thoroughbred stallions. One of those foals, Highland Code, belonged to Tom and Anne Durston-Smith who lived in Worcestershire. She was covered by the thoroughbred stallion, Lonesome Road. Eleven months later a colt was born. He would be called Highland Road, a fourth generation offspring from that foundation pony from the Isle of Rum. He was golden dun like his ancestor and, as time passed, it became clear that he was born with the star of Jupiter shining over him – the lucky star of destiny.

In the same year of Dorothy's obituary in 1984, I was reading the horses for sale advertisements in *Horse and Hound*, and I sat up. A heading had caught my eye.

Quality home bred dun 6 yr. old gelding by Lonesome Road.
7/8ths thoroughbred X 1/8th Highland pony. Riding club and Hunted.
Contact Tom Durston-Smith. Kyre Park. Tenbury Wells.

It was this mix of breeding that attracted me. Many of our British mountain and moorland ponies, and the Connemara ponies in Southern Ireland, are said to have existed on our islands since the Bronze and even the Ice age. They are tough and hardy, have a native cleverness, and a natural instinct to look after themselves. This near-thoroughbred horse had one eighth Highland pony in his breeding, and I had a strong urge to go and see it.

In contrast to our island's indigenous ponies, the evolution of the thoroughbred is more recent. Thoroughbred horses are the finest in the world. The blue-bloods of the equine species, and selectively bred for over 300 years for their speed, courage, and sheer ability. Their ancestry traces back to three stallions. The Darley Arabian, the Godolphin Arabian and the Byerley Turk, the latter mentioned at the beginning of this book. The Byerley Turk's story is told in detail by Jeremy James in his book of the same name. This horse was foaled in 1678 in the Balkans. Disciplined as a war horse, he carried his warrior archer in the battles of the Ottoman Empire. He was glossy bay in colour, and clearly an eye-catcher. The horse was captured at the siege of Buda in 1688 by the British army, and then acquired by Captain Robert Byerley of the 6th Dragoon Guards. As described earlier, he then joined the ranks of Orange King William as a charger, and sailed across the Irish Sea from Hoylake, where he fought bravely in the Battle of the Boyne. He was retired to stud at Goldsborough Hall in Yorkshire. This remarkable horse died in 1703 at the age of twenty-five. He was the first of the three foundation sires of today's racehorse. There is an arresting near life-size portrait of him which I have seen, in the Byerley Turk restaurant in county Kildare.

The Darley Arabian was born in the Syrian desert, amongst the nomadic tribes and tents of the Bedouin, and the Godolphin Arabian was born in Yemen; they were foaled in 1700 and 1724 respectively, and later imported to Britain. Galileo can trace his ancestry back to the Darley Arabian. The purity of the blood of the Arab horse was carefully guarded by the desert Arabs. They are known as Kehilan in Arabic, and this means thoroughbred. Under strict registration rules at Weatherbys, all thoroughbreds have the blood coursing through their veins of those two Arabian, and one Turk stallion. I hoped the horse advertised in *Horse and Hound* that day would have enough thoroughbred class, with a touch of native pony intelligence. My instinct was to be proved right.

I picked up the phone, and the next day Polly and I set forth to Lower House Farm, Kyre Park, and I remembered to push some notes in cash into my pocket. The countryside in this part of England, around Tenbury Wells, is typically green and leafy England with sheep grazing in the fields either side of the long drive, and horses standing nose to tail under parkland trees, swishing their tails. Tom led us into a neat farmyard, and I spotted Highland Road looking over his green-painted stable door. He turned his head as we approached, ears cocked in greeting. The look was bright and interested. I would describe his head as handsome, and I liked it immediately. It was a golden dun with a thin white blaze running the length of his face. He had biggish ears tipped with black, and his eyes were dark and broadly-set. Bred on the farm, the Durston-Smiths handled their young stock well, and Highland Road clearly liked people, and trusted them.

A frequent saying in horse parlance is 'no foot no horse'. The foot of a horse is like a box, and inside the hard outer horn are ligaments and the pedal and navicular bones; these bones are prone to arthritic inflammation of varying severity. The foot is the most common site of lameness in horses, and bruising and corns can be a problem, particularly on the thinner soles of thoroughbreds. With the fore-feet taking the full landing weight of a jumping horse, a good pair of front feet is essential. As I peered over the stable door I saw two perfectly-shaped, evenly-sized fore-feet, planted squarely and firmly on the stable floor.

Highland Road was led out of his stable. In some ways his physique was more pony than horse, although he measured just over 16 hands high. He was compact, and stood well over clean (as in unblemished) straight forelimbs. Tom got on him and trotted a few circles; with no warning Highland Road threw his head, nose vertical, towards the sky. Jumping up and down he was reluctant to go forward. It was a very different attitude to the friendly face that had greeted us from the stable. I felt a stab of disappointment but, determined to investigate further, suggested Polly ride off on a loose rein and experiment.

The horse soon relaxed. I was not expecting a Badminton horse, but I had a strong instinct that he just had something, and we were not witnessing it quite yet.

'Can we see him jump?' I said.

There was no arena, just a couple of poles and some hedges, ditches, and a drop off a bank. The hedges had bushed out through the summer months, and were tangled and hairy; they were not inviting. But by now Polly was cantering round the field and I bit my lip. With the promise of jumping, Highland Road had visibly grown in stature; his ears twitched back and forth as horses do in a form of conversation, and his eyes glowed and widened – as mine did a minute or two later. He looked twice the horse. Tom waved an arm and called to Polly, 'Jump that hedge and there is a ditch and bank with a drop over there, too.'

The pair cantered a circle and headed sharply towards the first hedge. Eyeing up the obstacle, the horse coiled himself, and flew – he was transformed. It was his total focus that impressed me, plus his natural balance and rhythm. My eyes followed him as he jumped from fence to fence. I felt he was genuine and intelligent, and my mind was made up – I liked enough of what I saw in this horse. I often relied on sixth sense, but I have made some mistakes. However, there was something about the way Highland Road had first greeted us in the stable yard. It was almost as if he knew us, and we had met before somewhere, but of course we hadn't. There are certain people, animals, and even houses that can leave a marked imprint on your life. We did not know it then, but Highland Road was going to be one of those animals.

The Durston-Smiths live in an attractive 17th century farmhouse where we looked at some photos of Highland Road as a foal with his dam – Highland Code. As we prepared to leave, I remembered the notes in my pocket. I did not want to risk anyone else having this horse.

'I would like to leave a deposit', I said. 'Subject to vet.'

'Oh, there is no need,' Tom answered.

However, it was agreed, and I drove home feeling secure that Highland Road would be ours.

We gave Highland Road the stable name Bumble, and he will be referred to by either name in this book. I am not sure how this name evolved; possibly, it was to do with his golden colour and black dorsal stripe, resembling a bee. Highland Road was a sociable horse, a happy personality, and trusting. He took an interest in everything going on, and was uncomplicated, so the other horses perhaps received more attention. But he didn't mind. He was just a generally easygoing chap. There followed nearly three years of horse and rider learning together. There were ups and downs, a broken collar bone, a splint (bony lump) on Bumble's near fore, a fall at a Junior trial at Witton Castle. But by 1986, with a promising second place at the Pony Club Championships, and Hubert Allfrey's eagle eye always alert, Polly was awarded a scholarship, funded by Subaru cars, to train with Mike and Angela Tucker, in the months building up to the 1987 Junior European Championships in Rome.

Mike and Angela were the best known husband and wife team synonymous with the sport of eventing. The familiar tones of Mike's BBC commentary from Badminton, Burghley, the World Equestrian Games and of course the Olympics, has been as much part of the entertainment as the competition itself. This does not only extend to eventing. At the 2012 Olympic Games in London, both the dressage and show jumping benefited from his enthusiastic and knowledgeable commentary.

Polly and Highland Road were now based in the golden circle of eventing, Tetbury in Gloucestershire, where she lived as family for ten months with Mike and Angela, and their two children, Andrew and Emma. Off she went to Gloucestershire and there, nearby, she has stayed to this day. Angela took care of most of Polly's training, interspersed with the valuable short courses for selected riders at team trainer Gill Watson's. Mike, too, played an important part. You have to know how to handle pressure, and the accompanying ups and downs. Mike kept Polly's mind focused on the positives, and the European Championships in Rome in September remained the target, but first we had to get through the Junior National Championships at Windsor in May, after which a long list for Rome would be announced.

A week before Windsor the phone rang in the hills of North Wales, and I listened to a very unhappy daughter.

'Bumble has a big leg. If we run him at Windsor the vet insists we will break him down.'

I knew Bumble's legs, they were good and hard. My instincts were full of doubt about what I had heard.

'Who has seen him?' I asked.

Polly named probably the best known vet in the competitive horse world at that time.

'Is there anyone else who can look at him? We must have a second opinion.'

'Well, Angela did mention someone called John Kilingbeck.'

'Get him right away,' I insisted.

I waited for news, and it was not long in coming. John Kilingbeck arrived at the Tuckers' that afternoon. They made their way to Bumble's stable, and the horse whickered, hoping for a polo-mint. Polly reached for a head collar and slipped it over his head. Together they entered the stable, and John looked hard at Bumble's forelegs. Then he crouched down and ran his hands up and down those same legs. Gently pressing, palpating, looking, feeling, flexing. After a while he straightened up, looked at Polly and said, pointing, 'Have you been putting anything on that leg?'

'Well yes,' replied Polly. 'He had a small cut and I have been poulticing it.'

John nodded and smiled.

'Well, Bumble has not got a "leg", there is nothing wrong with him, except that you have over treated the cut, and the poultice has had the effect of a blister. He will be fine for Windsor.'

When so much hangs on a decision like that, good news is overwhelming. John Kilingbeck has been Polly's vet ever since that day, nearly thirty years ago, and has seen our horses through Badminton, Burghley and many championships. I have no doubt that where the original long established vet, nearing his retirement, may have been a touch cursory with his opinion, John gave vital time and trouble to his examination. Bumble went to Windsor, performed impressively, and was included on the long list for the Junior European Championships in Rome.

Perhaps you are wondering, why was Bumble's leg not scanned? The answer is this. In 1987 veterinary scanning machines were barely in existence, if at all. It was all up to the veterinary surgeon's experience and expertise. John was quite a young vet in those days, but his expertise was in no doubt.

SIX

THE ROAD TO ROME

After Windsor, fourteen shortlisted riders competed at the final trial at Shamley Green in Hampshire, after which six horses would be selected for the British squad to travel to Rome for the European Championships early in September. The horses were stabled on site, and following the competition, strict instructions were given. No horse was to be visited once they had been settled for the night. Any extreme medication or walking horses during the night to mask stiffness or injury was forbidden. Early next morning there would be a vet's inspection, known as the 'trot up', which was scrutinised by team veterinary surgeon Bob Baskerville, Hubert Allfrey, team trainer Gill Watson and the selectors. There could be no risk of travelling six horses to Rome, only to be rejected by the Ground Jury in Italy for lack of soundness.

At nine o'clock the next morning fourteen anxious Juniors, with their horses and parents, gathered as one by one the horses were trotted up. Bumble was an expert, and he strode out well. Hubert Allfrey, Bob, Gill and the selectors then disappeared while we all waited. There was an edginess in the air and no one said much. Some people ambled away, and conversed in huddles. At last the group reappeared, and with a list in his hand Colonel Allfrey began to read.

'The squad of six for the 1987 Junior European Championships in Rome is as follows: Clare Bowley with Fair Share, William Fox-Pitt with Steadfast, Kristina Gifford with Song and Dance Man, Amanda Harwood with Razarda, Polly Lyon with Highland Road and Andrea Morris with Jack O' Lantern.'

There were disappointed faces and a few tears. Highland Road and Polly had won the final trial, so I was confident, but when I heard their name read out, the primary emotion was relief. There had been mistakes, frustrations and scratching of heads on this journey, but now we could relax just for a while, and plans for Rome could begin.

The squad was an interesting mix.

William Fox-Pitt was bred in the purple as far as eventing was concerned, with both parents having competed at Badminton. His 17hh horse was Steadfast; dark bay with a prominent white blaze and two white socks. He looked more suited to hunting over Irish banks, but he was true to his name, as he was to prove. Tina Gifford (later Cook) was the daughter of Josh Gifford, trainer of Grand National winner Aldaniti, and Althea Gifford, former International showjumper, so she, too, was bred for the job. Tina's horse was Song and Dance Man, an attractive smallish thoroughbred. Amanda Harwood, now Perrett, was the daughter of flat race trainer Guy Harwood. Amanda's horse, Raszarda, was a flamboyant and experienced part-bred grey Arab. Andrea Morris was a farmer's daughter from Bolton in Lancashire. Her horse, Jack O' Lantern, bright bay with a white face and two white stockings, would not have graced a show ring, but he had shown repeated consistency and deserved his place. Clare Bowley, farmer's daughter from Leicestershire, and protégée of former International Judy Bradwell, with her horse, Fair Share, an elegant bay thoroughbred.

There was a rumour that Judy had predicted, 'If Fair Share does not win an individual gold for Britain, then no one is likely to.'

Finally, Polly Lyon from North Wales, father a solicitor and mother a British Horse Society instructor. Polly's horse, Highland Road, a seven-eighths thoroughbred X one-eighth Highland pony; a golden dun colour with black zebra stripes on his forelegs, and biggish ears.

The six horses set forth on a four day road journey to Italy, travelling in two horse-boxes with their grooms and Gill Watson, also acting as chef d'équipe. They arrived with three free days to acclimatise the horses to the baking hot climate. The riders followed by air with Colonel Bill Lithgow, who was to take over as Junior chairman from Hubert Allfrey. A large and enthusiastic band of supporters travelled from Britain and amongst them, and joining Christopher and me, were my sister and brother-in-law Lois and Barry Edwards, and our friends and sponsors of Polly, Christopher and Hilary Banner. Tory took time out from her job in London and flew to Rome to support her sister.

The Centro Equestre Federale, at Pratoni del Vivaro, is fifteen miles south of Rome, and was the scene of the Rome Olympic Games in 1960. It is now the national training centre for Italy's top equestrians. The area is set amongst rolling hills with forest in the distance. Based on volcanic ash, this provided perfect going for the horses. Views of the cross-country were excellent, the stables cool and airy, and the facilities for spectators included several good restaurants. We took the opportunity of a trip to St. Peters and the Castel del Gandolfo, but I can recall very little, my mind totally taken up with what would happen in the next few days at Pratoni del Vivaro.

For nearly twenty years I had been hands on with the ponies and horses that had dominated our lives, from hunting through the winter, and gymkhana and Pony Club in the summer, to the more serious Pony Club eventing, and then the nearly professional business of British team selection. I had ridden 12hh ponies to 16.2hh horses, mucked out, cleaned the tack, driven the horse box, walked courses, booked the blacksmith, called the vet and done the endless entries, registrations and so on. It was, of course, a labour of love and years of tremendous fun; but here in Rome, decisions regarding Polly and Highland Road were not mine to be made. They were part of the British squad. They had a timetable for each day, Polly had her own allocated groom, and Bob Baskerville checked each horse several times daily. Overseeing the riders and the horses, and in charge, were trainer Gill Watson and Colonel Bill Lithgow. With all horses passing the inspection on the Wednesday, the serious business of winning medals – preferably gold – began in earnest.

The team of four was Clare, Kristina, Andrea and Polly. William and Amanda would ride as individuals. After two days of dressage in dazzling sunshine, Polly finished in second place just behind Martina Kruemmel of Germany, with William third. The German team stood in first place after those two days. Saturday's cross-country would be crucial. The Brits needed to catch up with Germany. As third British team member to go and with temperatures soaring to 80 degrees Fahrenheit, Bumble waited his turn in the cool of his stable to start the first phase of roads and tracks, Phase A. Bumble's temperament was essentially laid back and as he mooched round waiting for his turn, I saw Gill head quickly over to Polly.

'Come on, Polly, wake him up a bit.'

Gill had eyes everywhere, and was keeping a watch out for all her charges. Polly's second place at that point could clinch a team medal, and they duly obliged with a faultless cross-country inside the time; but the Germans too had gone well, and held their leading place.

Sunday dawned in a sweltering heat. Germany remained in a strong gold medal position, with two show jumps in hand over Britain in second place, while Italy snapped at the British heels in third. Polly retained her place in individual silver medal position just behind Martina Kruemmel. Set in a hollow, the showjumping arena glowed green in contrast to the parched grass surrounding, and far away the hills shimmered in a hot blue haze. Tubs of flowers framed the brightly painted fences, and beside the arena was a long table covered in a royal blue velvet cloth edged in gold. Laid on this was an impressive display of silver cups, trophies and rosettes. Spectators arrived and crowded the ropes, several standing on the bank at one end. There was a festive air with music playing in the background. The Italians were putting on a good show and wanted everyone to enjoy themselves. Dominating the arena on one side, and soaring up to a cloudless blue sky, flew the bright colours of the flags of all eight nations taking part. These were Italy, Ireland, Great Britain, Holland, France, Hungary, Poland and West Germany.

The showjumping always takes place in reverse order of merit. This left Polly last but one to go before Martina Kruemmel. With over forty riders to jump there would be a long wait. Nerves began to tell, poles rolled in the arena. There were worried faces in the British camp. Clear rounds were needed. Time marched on, and at last Polly went to mount Bumble, waiting in the shade of the trees with his groom, Sandra Limbrick. From an early hectic practice arena, noisy with thudding hooves, sharp instructions called in a variety of languages, and horses jostling for places to jump, gradually one by one the arena emptied, and it became very quiet. The final two, Polly and Martina, circled round, waiting to be called. Gill was there helping Polly, but she knew Bumble did not need much practice. He knew his job.

Clare and Fair Share produced a vital clear round, and with poles down from the German team, the British had overtaken them, and squeezed into first place. But only just – there was not a fence between them. There could be no mistakes. Polly had to jump clear to secure a gold medal for the British team, and she knew it. She was under pressure. A clear round also guaranteed her second place and an individual silver medal. Standing together I saw our bunch of sponsor and family supporters; I could imagine their tension.

Please Bumble, go clear, travelled through my mind.

Then I walked away quickly, to watch from afar. Under the trees a crowd had gathered, the rest of the British squad, plus Gill, Bill

Lithgow, Mike and Angela Tucker, Bob, grooms, parents, just about everybody quiet and still, all eyes on Polly and Bumble.

A hush descended as they cantered into the arena. Bumble's coat gleamed in the sunshine; he looked splendid, but there was a dark patch of sweat on his neck. He had picked up the tension. They halted opposite the judge's box, and Polly saluted with her whip and a nod of her head. The bell rang, she circled once, and set off towards the first fence. I simply could not look. Just glancing up every so often, I tried not to listen, but there was complete silence, just the rhythmic canter drum of Bumble's hooves on the firm, green turf.

'Be-de-boom, be-de-boom, be-de-boom.'

A dog barked far away in the distance. No one moved. Nearly halfway round, and they were still clear. A difficult treble coming up, and with knees near his chin, Bumble pinged through with feet to spare. Now it was the final fence. A hundred eyes and more were fixed on horse and rider. But Polly was in her own world, just she and her horse, oblivious of anyone or anything except the shiny coloured obstacle looming ahead. She gave Bumble a nudge of the spur, he accelerated and gathered himself. And then, as in a flashback, I saw him as I had that very first time three years ago, jumping an overgrown hedge in a farm field far away in England. But here we were in Italy, a Union Jack on his saddle cloth, jumping for Britain, about to clinch a gold medal, and it was just the same horse. Complete focus, coiled like a spring, and he *flew*. The silence broke, the British camp erupted. Bumble galloped through the finish, and Polly stuck her arm up in triumph.

'Clear within the time.'

The official result echoed over the tannoy. The British team had triumphed, and they were ecstatic. It had been a close run thing and a great team victory.

But wait! As Polly left the arena beaming with relief, another rider entered. It was not all over yet. Martina Kruemmel, the final competitor, was already cantering round waiting for the bell. The German team had slipped to a silver medal position, but Martina, and her horse Waldfee, were riding for gold – individual gold.

Once again silence fell, the bell rang, and the pair cantered towards the first fence. The atmosphere was mesmeric. Tory and I were now standing together. I was still in recovery, but Tory had her 'eye on the ball'. Waldfee was ebony black and a horse of exceptional quality. As always, Bumble had given the fences feet, but this horse was giving them yards. I turned to Tory and said, 'This isn't going to touch a thing.'

She nodded, not looking at me, eyes still fixed on the horse and rider in the arena. They continued fence after fence. And then I heard it. An audible intake of breath, a great gasp from the watching spectators, and Tory's quick voice beside me.

'She's *missed* it – she's missed the fence.'

It was incredible but so she had. Staring into the arena I saw Martina turn back, and re-approach the missed fence. She had sailed straight past the jump before the treble. But did she cross her tracks or not? If so, there would be penalties, but with more fences to jump, no final result had been given. There was whispered confusion and excited babbling outside the arena. Martina cantered through the finish, dejection written all over her face, and the British waited in suspense once more. Then it came –the official result – first in Italian.

'Martina Kruemmel et Waldfee, dieci penalita.' Then in English, 'Martina Kruemmel and Waldfee, ten penalties.'

This was unbelievable. Polly had helped clinch the team gold with a final clear round, and now, with the hand of fate, she had achieved the double, and won the individual gold as well. It was devastating for poor Martina – what a thing to happen. It had relegated the German team and her individually to bronze. Italy, the host nation, had come up to team silver, and a delighted William had overtaken Martina to take individual silver.

Sportingly the German team shook hands all round, and the Polly/Highland Road support group ran over and mingled with the excitement. There followed a parade of mounted competitors. The band struck up with Meyerbeer's Coronation March as the riders came proudly past us. Then they lined up facing the array of gold, silver and bronze, and the prize-giving commenced. The scene was one of relaxed jollity with people in summer clothes, cotton shirts, panama hats, and amongst the Italian officials, formal linen suits. An elegant Italian gentleman in the presentation group removed his bowler hat, and gave Gill a congratulatory kiss on both cheeks. Medals were presented. The British flag was raised, and God Save the Queen rang out.

Then came a special moment in my story. There were to be a few more, but for now it was Polly and Bumble in Rome. The two were ushered forward, with Gill beside them. A hush fell and I heard the tannoy.

'The winner of these Championships: Gold medal, and the Junior European Champions of 1987 – for Great Britain – Polly Lyon and Highland Road.'

Once more the National Anthem played, this time for these two – the golden dun horse and astride him Polly, standing out together. Slowly the Union Jack made its way to the top of the white pole for the second time, Bumble nodded sleepily in the sun, and Polly gazed up at the ascending flag. William, standing just behind with Steadfast, removed his hat. I glanced over at our loyal band of family and friends. They stood quietly together again, no agonising suspense this time, but a couple of grown men with a tear or two glinting in their eyes.

Burghley Horse Trials was held the same week as the Junior Championships in Rome. The news of the British triumph in Italy came through to the press office on site. Pooch Spiller, Flint and Denbigh hunt secretary, was helping in the scorer's marquee, and picked up the news first. Running out of the tent and waving a piece of paper she called out, 'The British have won in Rome and Polly Lyon has won Gold.'

At Christmas time we had a party at Pen Parc for Flint and Denbigh supporters to celebrate the success. We could not let Bumble miss out, and with champagne corks popping and people cheering, Polly led him through the door of the house and into the dining room with a gold medal round his ears. Unfazed, he ambled across the carpet, and reached out to grab a piece of Christmas tree.

Christopher and I had travelled to Rome by car over four days, serenaded by Luciano Pavarotti. Now whenever I hear the great tenor I am reminded of a brilliant blue sky, pasta and chianti, camaraderie and a soaring Union Jack. Italian voices over a tannoy, and a gold medal twinkling in the rays of a scorching sun.

The Italian press gave the event wide coverage, and an Italian girl, aged about twelve, had devoured the news of the home team's silver medals. She had also fallen under the spell of the British horse who won double gold in Rome. Like Dorothy MacKenzie, who had wished for a little dun pony from the isle of Rum, this young girl wished that she, too, could own a horse like Highland Road, and we know that Dorothy MacKenzie's wish had come true. The girl's name was Laura.

SEVEN

ZONHOVEN – YOUNG RIDER
EUROPEAN CHAMPIONSHIPS 1988

Polly and Highland Road held the Junior European Championship title, but proving themselves at the next level – the Young Riders – would not be a shoo-in. Selection trials followed the same pattern but at Advanced level. Heading the selection panel was chairman Christopher Schofield OBE. Over the years I got to know Christopher well; he was a delightful man, and a familiar figure at many horse trials in traditional tweed cap and green Husky jacket. Very tall – well over six feet – he had an authoritative air, but he was fair and encouraging with quite a twinkling eye. Throughout his sixteen years as chairman, his strike rate for Young Rider gold medals was extremely high. His expectations from his Young Riders were equally so. We had the first taste of this at Polly's first trial, which was held in the grounds of Belton Park in Lincolnshire, a prestige event and used as a pre Badminton warm up.

The water fence was approached through dark trees. Unseen until the last minute, the water glinted and took horses by surprise. Horses are wary going from light into dark, their feral instincts warning them there may be a tiger waiting to pounce. I ran to my preplanned vantage point as Bumble and Polly set off. Within earshot of the loudspeaker I waited for horse and rider to come into view, when over the tannoy came, 'We believe Polly Lyon has had a stop at the water, but she is over at the second attempt.'

Damn! I thought, *twenty penalties.* I began to walk back to the horse box, disappointed, but then stopped to listen again. Fellow team gold medallist Clare Bowley and her horse, Fair Share, were not far behind; through the tannoy I heard, 'Clare Bowley has had a fall, but she is up on her feet and the horse has been caught.'

That would be sixty penalties, and I breathed rather an unsporting sigh of relief. Polly was not the only one of Christopher Schofield's rising stars to have had a blob at their first trial.

After the prize-giving, at which neither Polly nor Clare would be taking part, the chairman asked the pair to come and see him. I waited, and eventually both girls reappeared, looking distinctly unamused.

'You have both won gold medals, but that was last year; you will have to do better to merit a place on my Young Rider squad.'

Strong words, but behind those words Christopher had their best interests at heart.

With fortunes improving, the Young Rider National Championships, held at the ancestral home of the Lane-Fox family, Bramham Park in Yorkshire, duly arrived. Highland Road always did his best to please, but I would not say he was an especially competitive horse. His touch of Highland pony breeding gave him an easygoing nature, and life in the fast lane was not always his scene. Highland ponies were, after all, employed to plod down hillsides with a stag slung over their backs.

A respected horseman of the old school, Mr. Gibson, said to me he preferred horses with steady temperaments rather than the fizz-pops.

'On the whole,' said he, 'rousing a horse up is easier than winding them down.'

Bumble's attitude across country was clever and genuine but he required switching on and positive riding. He was, however, an ace show jumper. Twisting in the air like a circus tumbler, he would turn himself inside out rather than touch those coloured poles.

Angela Tucker had given Polly much help before the dressage, and as Highland Road cantered round waiting for the bell, with his golden dun colour and shiny black legs, and Polly, sitting tall and elegant in top hat and tails, I was optimistic. Steps rhythmic as a drum beat, head steady, neck arched, there was true harmony, and the pair shot to the top of the leader board, and stayed there. With Polly keeping her foot down on the cross-country course the next day, they completed well inside the time, and with two fences in hand as they entered the showjumping arena, only a disaster would prevent victory. But there were no mistakes, the pair finished thirteen marks ahead of a competitive field, and became the 1988 Young Rider National Champions. Bumble had moved up a grade with spectacular aplomb. He was also a very sound horse who regularly produced trouble-free inspections by the Ground Jury. How different this was from Polly's next Young Rider challenge, two years later. But this would be with a different horse.

The 1988 Young Rider European Championships were held in Zonhoven in Belgium, and as the time grew near, Bumble showed a change in his attitude. The nub of it was he was getting fitter, and rather cocky. After Bramham he returned to Pen Parc for a holiday, and was then brought up for the preliminary road work. Polly was away, and it was up to me to proceed with this early fittening work. Bumble was an enjoyable ride, setting his head and swinging up the steep Welsh hills in a spanking trot with ease. Approaching home, I heard a lorry groaning up behind, and moved over to let it pass. Our well-mannered, good-natured horse decided to take the lorry on. With his ears flat back – this was so unusual, he never laid his ears back –he leapt into the road, gave a determined double-barrel at the slowly passing vehicle, and clattered along the tarmac in a series of bone-shaking fits and starts. This horse was clearly taking on the mantle of number one. How dare that lorry overtake him.

But this was not all; Bumble reverted to his trick of jumping up and down in juddering jerks with his nose pointing to the clouds. A repetition of the first day we saw him at the Durston-Smiths. He cannily realised that if he timed this party piece when the bell rang before a dressage test, there was absolutely nothing Polly could do except drop the reins, leave Bumble to have his say, and pray that he would then enter the arena. He had also started to grind his teeth. The sound is unmistakable – like the crunching of gears. Teeth grinding is considered a resistance, as is repeated swishing of a tail, and he could be marked down by the dressage judges. Every mark counts, and we discovered the trick was to smear soap – just a little – along his teeth. He didn't much like it, but it worked, and he had plenty of Polo mints afterwards. Bumble was primarily equable in temperament, but he possessed plenty of character.

So from Italy 1987, it was to Belgium 1988 that we set forth with sponsors and family once more. There is great camaraderie and team spirit on these trips abroad. The objective for the British team is always the same. To pull out all the stops, ride at the top of your game and produce medals – preferably the colour of gold.

Zonhoven in Belgium did not have the romantic ring of Rome, but there was anticipated excitement all the same. The championships were situated on a vast expanse of flat, tree-studded heathland near to a busy commuter area. Brightly coloured advertising boards and sponsors' logos indicated commercial involvement at the event. Set below tiered grandstands with a choice of restaurants and bars, the arenas presented excellent viewing. Christopher, Tory and our sponsors Christopher and Hilary Banner, along with my sister Lois, brother-in-law Barry and nephew Charles, soon set up camp here with tables, chairs and a large stripey umbrella. Over the five days of competition there was a holiday atmosphere, the wine flowed and they were set to enjoy themselves. Hanging in the air was the prospect of the British team as medal winners and, as National Champions, the possibility of Polly Lyon and Highland Road producing a repeat of Rome.

Flags of thirteen countries were represented. The British team were William Fox-Pitt and Steadfast, Pippa Nolan – later Funnell – and Sir Barnaby, Susanna McCaire and Master Marius, and Polly and Highland Road. Clea Hoeg and Clare Bowley would ride as individuals. With the Germans more than twenty points ahead after two days of dressage, we had the usual catching up to do. Meticulous planning from Christopher Schofield and Gill Watson on cross-country day became crucial. The course weaved in and out between tall silver birch trees and several jumps were met on a turn. It was proving difficult to keep the foot on the accelerator, and time faults were racking up. The faster you go, the greater risk you take for a jumping error. It could be a fall, or a bad approach resulting in a stop or a run out. The team strategy had now become one of fast and clear, rather than a slower but safe option and time faults. In other words, the Brits must throw caution to the winds and 'go for it'.

In the ten minute box I noticed an air of fevered consternation at the British base, where Christopher and Henry Nicoll were studying the results coming in. Clearly not all was going to plan. I waited for Polly to trot into the box after Phase C, the second roads and tracks. Sure enough here she was, spot on time. Bumble's two grooms ran over to cool him down. But first, all horses were checked by the veterinary surgeon ready and waiting with his stethoscope. With his heart rate and everything fine, Polly handed him to the two girls and strode over to Gill for the vital briefing on how the course was riding. Pippa and Sir Barnaby had had a problem – which was eventually over-ruled, but not till much later – and there were some formidable performers from other nations yet to come. To stay in contention something had to be done. Polly listened carefully as Gill detailed what was required. It did not take long.

'You have to go clear, Polly, and the time is tight.'

The clock ticked, and I heard the steward call out, 'No 19, one minute.'

Polly at the ready was legged up; she gave Bumble a reassuring pat on his neck, and he trotted into the start box, ears pricked, eyes huge. The starter held up his watch. Bumble tensed his neck and danced, he knew what to expect.

'5 – 4 – 3 – 2 – 1 *Go.*'

Polly set her chin, leant forward, gave Bumble a squeeze, and he shot out of the start box. *Whoosh* – away they went, and I watched his muscled quarters and black tail disappear into the trees, my stomach churning.

The Colonels and Christopher Schofield.

Gill Watson briefing Polly. Heart check for Highland Road.

Only three competitors completed clear inside the time that day. Bumble had galloped helter-skelter round the twisty track, zipping in and out of the tall silver birch trees, with Polly keeping her foot to the boards, to record the fastest time of the day. Not only did this put the British into top spot in front of the Germans and Swedes, who were now neck and neck, but Polly had pulled herself up from fifth in the dressage – where Bumble had threatened his naughty party piece – and into the lead individually.

Designed to provide maximum suspense for the spectators, Highland Road, in top spot, would be last to go in the show jumping. Just one fence down could ruin the party. Could Polly possibly strike gold again? Once more I could not watch, and striding away from the arena as the penultimate rider completed, I went and hid in one of the line of mobile loos. However, I could still hear. But you cannot hear silence. There were no groans, no 'ooohs' and 'aaahs', no crashing of poles. The only sound came at the end. I heard it loud and clear. Cheers and applause told me everything, and I ran out and over to the arena. The British team had triumphed, and the pair had won double gold again. Highland Road had the unique distinction of being the only horse at that time to hold Junior and Young Rider titles consecutively, and to top it all, they had now qualified for Badminton.

It was twenty-three years since my pony Heidi had won a first rosette at a Welsh country show on the side of a mountain.

With extensive publicity in the local press we found further sponsorship from two companies based in North Wales. T. Norbury and Company was a local printing firm headed by Flint and Denbigh hunting enthusiast, and friend of the family, Michael Norbury. Ifor Williams Trailers was based in the depths of the Denbighshire hills. Company chief Ifor Williams spoke only Welsh, and had a reputation for keeping a tight fist on the purse strings, but Polly managed to charm him and his directors – who did speak English – and they too joined the team.

British squad, from left William Fox-Pit, Polly and Highland Road, Pippa Funnell, Susanna McCaire.

EIGHT

THE AINTREE CHALLENGE –
PREPARATIONS FOR BADMINTON

A chance to compete at Badminton, the premier event in the world, is the dream of many, but the opportunity for the few. Highland Road was an Advanced horse with a Young Rider National and European Championship under his belt. Nevertheless, there were some who considered him too much of a pony to tackle the toughest course on the eventing calendar. They had a point and I was fully aware of this myself. At nineteen Polly was eligible for another two years in Young Riders. Should we save Bumble and go for a double, or even a treble? But I was convinced we must grab this opportunity, as another could take a long time in coming, and might never come at all. Badminton 1989 must be the target.

Mike and Angela Tucker played an important role during Polly's build-up to Badminton. Close at hand were veterinary surgeon John Kilingbeck and farrier Bernie Tidmarsh. Bernie Tidmarsh is a renowned farrier throughout the profession. At that time he was regular blacksmith to the Beaufort Hunt horses, and won the best shod competition at Gatcombe Park on every occasion that I can remember. Bumble was kingpin in the stable yard, and he knew it. He had the glow of a champion. However, like all intense preparations for major events, not everything goes to plan – in fact on this occasion, things could hardly have been worse.

After Zonhoven, Bumble came home to the hills of North Wales for several weeks holiday. Turned out in the fields around Pen Parc he munched away contentedly, and lay sprawled on the warm grass in the late autumn sunshine. As the days grew shorter and a chill set in, he grew a thick winter coat, dense and waterproof like his Highland ancestors, while his waistline was carefully watched. In January he was brought up from the fields, clipped of his furry coat, and boxed up for the long journey back to Gloucestershire to prepare for the 1989 season and Badminton.

At home in Wales, that pesky phone rang one evening. It was late, and I jumped, expecting a problem.

'Hello, everything OK?'

'Well, Mark Phillips has just rung,' said Polly. 'He wants me to take part in a celebrity challenge in aid of the Injured Jockeys Fund, and the Mark Davies Injured Riders Appeal.'

'Oh, that sounds interesting,' I said unsuspecting, wondering why she had rung at that hour to tell me this. There was a pause and then she said, 'I'd better explain. Mark has this idea of six top National Hunt jockeys riding round the Advanced course at Gatcombe, and six International eventers taking part in a race round one circuit of the Grand National course.'

Staring at me on the wall beside the phone was a Cecil Aldin print of horses tumbling and sprawling into the notorious ditch at Becher's Brook, named after Captain Becher, who landed in the brook during the early days of the race. My antennae were now on high alert. I had guessed what was coming.

'All this will be pre-recorded and shown on BBC Grandstand on Grand National day as a build-up to the racing. He wants me to take part as one of the eventers.'

My reaction was immediate.

'You must be mad. What will you ride? And you've got Badminton to tackle in just over three weeks.'

'Well, I've decided I'm going to do it,' was the reply.

Absolutely no point in arguing, and I had to admit to a sneaking temptation for the challenge.

'Apparently a horse can be provided.'

Oh no, I thought. *No way were we going to end up with any old moke.*

Perhaps that is unfair to the organisers, but decided 'the devil you know...'

'You'd better take Buckspinner.' With that the conversation ended, and replacing the phone, I kicked myself for not putting my foot down, but now it was too late.

Buckspinner was a horse we owned who had previously raced in point-to-points. A nearly black, very handsome horse by Politico, sire of Grand National winner Party Politics, he had the credentials to tackle a big jump, but he was not the snappiest over a fence. The die was now cast, and we prepared to travel to Gatcombe to watch the National Hunt jockeys in the first of the two challenges. The list of contenders was impressive.

Ace jockey Richard Dunwoody, Steve Smith Eccles, Graham McCourt, Brendan Powell, champion jockey Peter Scudamore, and Desert Orchid's pilot Simon Sherwood. These were some of the best jockeys in the country, but they were used to jumping steeplechase fences very fast with many other horses bumping and galloping along upsides, fighting it out to the finishing post. It is a world away from jumping solid timber as quick as you dare, down sheer drops, and into lakes. Galloping within a herd is instinctive to horses, and racing comes more naturally to them than eventing. Either way to get the top spot you must keep your foot on the fast pedal, and the margin for error is nail-bitingly small, as we were to discover.

Our trip to Aintree for the second phase of the Barbour/Seagram sponsored challenge came the Sunday before Grand National day, April 2nd 1989. By now plenty of publicity had reached the press as well as amongst the Flint and Denbigh hunting and Pony Club fraternity at home. An enthusiastic band of supporters, including our sponsors Christopher Banner and Ifor Williams Trailers, set forth for Aintree on a wet, windy and cold day. The other five eventers were Olympic gold medallist Mark Todd, Badminton winners Ian Stark and Rodney Powell, and Senior British team members Robert Lemieux and Madeleine Gurdon – the latter of whom was one day to bag a millionaire and become the future Lady Lloyd Webber. Christopher and I arriving at the famous racecourse, and finding ourselves in the hallowed area of weighing rooms, jockeys' changing rooms, officials and hospitality areas, was a complete haze. I tried to locate Polly and Buckspinner. There were people milling round, mobile BBC cameras, ambulance and horse transport. We had complimentary lunch tickets, but I could not face anything to eat. The rain was relentless, the clock ticked by and nerves jangled.

At 1.45pm we began to prepare Buckspinner. Polly was already kitted up – blue silk over her crash hat. Horses were given a final check, and a few nervous quips could be heard coming from Mark and Ian's stables. Buck was trembling like a leaf, staring wide-eyed into the distance. He sensed something was up. He would never have jumped fences like these before, and neither had Polly. At 2.15pm I led him out and legged Polly into the saddle. Leaning down and running her finger down the girth she said, 'Quickly, can you tighten my girth again?'

I fiddled with the over girth, and hung grimly on to Buckspinner's head, as he wheeled round like a dervish. Dodging his leaping hooves I hauled on the saddle girth, missed the buckle, and felt a searing pain like fire shoot down my back. '*Youch!* But too bad,' I reacted, and hauled again harder, this time successfully. With that, the pair of them spun round and galloped off down the Aintree sward. I watched them disappearing into the sheet of rain, and thought what a powerful back end Buckspinner had.

Hurriedly I made my way to the course. In the distance I saw six horses circling, and the starter on his rostrum, a flag down by his side. Then I noticed the ambulance, and behind it the large green cross of the horse ambulance, both slowly making their way towards the horses and riders, ready to track them round the course. Three or four cars followed, including the BBC cameras with Richard Pitman, commentator, and Mark Phillips in a Range Rover with a car load. This included Christopher, who, like me, had been offered the ride. I declined, preferring to be on my own.

Fear, excitement, glory or despair, what would it be and why do we do it? It's that five percent over the ninety-five. It is because of the thrill of success you can look back on over a lifetime, with a smile and a catch at your heart. The despair and disappointment you must turn the page and shut away in the attic.

I checked my watch and stared into the mist. The rain wet my face, I was cold and shivered. Less than a minute to go. I saw the horses lining up and the starter raise his arm. The flag fluttered in the breeze, then down it came. This was it. They were off. Staring at the ground, I started to pace, and so began the tortuous wait. Huge fences ahead with iconic names. Becher's Brook, Valentine's Brook, the Canal Turn. What would happen out there? Would all the horses finish? Would one of them be Buckspinner? I checked my watch again, and then again; the glass face, like my own, streaked with rain, the ticking hands obscured. I peered into the distance. Where were they? Surely I should see them by now. Then through the grey mist, ghostly shapes loomed into view. At speed they came. Shielding my eyes I counted.

'One – Two – Three – Four. *Four* – there should be *six*.'

I searched for Polly's blue colours. No sign. I checked again but there was no Buckspinner and no Polly. My heart by now in my boots,

I suddenly saw it, the shape of the ambulance driving at speed, and in the distance was a horse being led, and I recognised the dark outline of Buckspinner and with him, Flint and Denbigh hunting friend, Sue Hunter. The ambulance driver spotted me running and drew to a halt. Christopher was in the passenger seat. He instantly reassured me, 'She's OK.' The coiled wire in my stomach eased, and going round to the back the door was opened and I climbed in. Polly was laid out, and a support collar was fixed around her neck.

'Is Buck alright?' she asked, leaning up on her elbow.

'Yes, I have just seen him being led back, what happened?'

'Well, he leapt off in front as soon as the flag went down. He took a strong hold and I let him have his head. We were going well, and jumped the Canal Turn still ahead. I was aware when Becher's was coming up, and I was ready for it. Buck met the fence on a perfect stride, and we soared. It looked massive on the walk round, and it felt just as massive when we jumped it. Then just three fences from home, at the twelfth, it's a blank. I don't remember a thing after that.'

'Well, you were not the only one to tip up,' I tried to comfort her. 'Rodney Powell and Pomeroy hit the deck too.'

After the drama of the two challenges, the jockeys and eventers came out equal as the jockeys had had two fallers at Gatcombe as well. Not long afterwards, I was able to watch the recording, and saw indeed that Buckspinner was eating up the fences. I have a unique photograph of them jumping Becher's before it was modified, as it has been today. The press report in *Horse and Hound* said: *Polly Lyon got just a bit too enthusiastic riding around the Grand National course in the Barbour/ Seagram challenge, where she had a spectacular wipe-out and injured her neck.*

The preparations for Badminton now began in earnest. With Highland Road's one-eighth pony blood in his otherwise thoroughbred breeding, he would need to be supremely fit. Polly put him on a rigorous programme of diet and interval training. Interval training is a form of timed fitness work used by, amongst others, racehorse trainer Martin

Pipe and Olympic middle distance runner Sebastian Coe. Lucinda Prior-Palmer was one of the early pioneers of this method for event horses. Bumble's food was carefully weighed out. He had regular blood tests. Polly boxed him up to hills twice a week. So much can go wrong in the final stages of a major event as the fast work builds up to a peak. Those elite horses were like high performance machines, but with a beating heart and a sometimes questioning mind. Bumble was always a smiley kind of horse, but as he became super fit he became tetchy, laying back his ears when his feed arrived. He was, of course, on a permanent diet, and hunger makes the most amicable person grouchy. But this was a good sign, because a touch of the 'mean' streak in this naturally friendly horse was needed to tackle Badminton's ferocious fences.

The plan was to complete three prep competitions during the build-up, but torrential rain fell that spring, followed by the highly contagious equine herpes virus. Events were cancelled everywhere, including the Advanced tracks at Brigstock and Brockenhurst. Missing a single prep was manageable, but two was a disaster. It left Polly in a desperate state of worry and nerves. She also had recurring pain in her neck from the fall at Aintree. I travelled down to Tetbury immediately. Solutions had to be found and fast. First there was a phone call to Swindon osteopath John Skull, renowned for mending National Hunt jockeys quickly. Secondly, and crucially, how could Bumble, and for that matter Polly too, get some confidence-giving serious fences under their belt before Badminton? With my mind in overdrive on the journey to Tetbury, I had a memory jolt. Of course! Mark Phillips's words to Polly when presenting her with the Range Rover bursary she had won at Olympia in December. 'If I can ever be of help, let me know.'

'Polly!' I said. 'Ring Mark – remember what he said to you at Olympia, ring him, I'm sure he will help.'

And that was how Bumble, Polly and I found ourselves at Gatcombe Park a few days later, helping to shoo sheep off the cross-country course with Mark Phillips, and Mark casually pointing to several of the

Advanced fences partially set up for the British Championships later that year, and instructing Polly to 'just pop round those.'

This was no ordinary schooling session. Jumping unflagged obstacles of these dimensions in cold blood was a strong test. As Mark and I followed in a Land Rover, undulating over the terrain with a dog at my feet, I thought silently, *this exercise could be make or break*. But such was the rapport horse and rider had with each other, they jumped round with ease. I am absolutely certain that Mark's help that day put the vital edge to Polly's belief in her horse, that he could, and would jump Badminton's massive obstacles.

After Bumble's school round Gatcombe until the longed-for day of arrival at Badminton, he was watched and treated like the Crown Jewels. Polly checked his legs several times a day. His breathing and recovery rate after galloping was carefully monitored. We were on the edge of our seats. We had got this far. The weeks of preparation had had their scares, but now all was ready, and the omens looked good.

NINE

BADMINTON

Inspiration – the foundation of all human progress

The inscription on the Leverhulme
memorial at Port Sunlight Wirral

The little village of Badminton in Gloucestershire, with its traditional lime-washed cottages, is picture-postcard attractive. Normally a quiet country hamlet, during the week of Badminton it is heaving with 4 x 4s, horse boxes – many with foreign names and logos splashed across the side, and some the size of bungalows on wheels – beautiful elite horses, a myriad of people all involved on the same mission; everyone and everything connected with the great event. There are trusty grooms lumping mountains of kit, the clink of iron on iron from the farriers, hot steel hissing as horse shoes are dunked in water, and vets with estate car boots packed with every equine medical aid. There are equine trainers, human trainers, medical teams, press, policemen and the cream of the world's competitors, plus their supporters, speaking in tongues of many languages from around the globe. The place is throbbing with pent-up expectation and excitement.

That was the scene before us as we drove into the village and the competitor's park, and pulled down the ramp. Bumble paused at the top, looked about him, and then clopped out of the horse box. Every horse was checked in by stud groom Brian Higham. He ran his finger down the list in his hand.

'Ah yes, Polly,' he said. 'Number 50, Highland Road, you are in Badminton House stables.'

We were lucky. Bumble had been allocated one of the spacious indoor stables housed within the historic Cotswold stone buildings that make up the great stable yard of the estate, with its impressive clock tower and high sculptured archways.

As Young Rider National and European Champions, the pair had been given positive press coverage. Polly walked the four mile cross-country course four or five times, twice with the Tuckers, and then on her own, picking up tips from other more experienced campaigners on the way round. Mike was commentating on cross-country day for the BBC, and Angela herself was competing. Every step of the course and the thirty-one fences she would gallop and jump was planned. Practically every blade of grass, every tree noted. When to press the accelerator, kick on, and make up time, when to give Bumble a breather, when to collect him up into a short stride, and when to drive on into a powerful gallop for a towering hedge and ditch. There were two that year, appropriately named Becher's and Aintree, with vast yawning ditches. Every fence was scrutinised at every angle for approach, terrain, distance of strides and landing. Fence nine presented a sheer drop of up to six feet six inches, depending on where you landed, followed immediately by high bounce rails – these are a double of fences with no stride in between, requiring athleticism and quick thinking from the horse. Probably the biggest 'rider frightener' was the Vicarage V. Huge angled rails over a cavernous ditch, which remains unchanged as part of the course today. Bold riding and a superglue seat was crucial. All those years of pony hunting, up mountains and down dingles with the Flint and Denbigh hounds, would stand Polly in good stead.

After the vet's inspection on Wednesday, while the riders study the course in meticulous detail, there are thousands of spectators gazing at the fences from behind the ropes, and wandering round the park, relaxed, interested and enjoying themselves. Thursday and Friday are dressage days, and the scene around the practice arenas is one of elegance and concentration, in rather a sedate, albeit highly charged atmosphere. Horses plaited and groomed to perfection, and riders in top hat and tails, several proudly carrying their country's flags, stitched neatly onto their jackets. Some people wear crash hats now too – 'elf 'n' safety', I expect. I am not sure they look quite right with a tail coat. There is nothing more pleasing to the eye than beautiful horses, and slim riders – you hope, in top hat and tails, gliding gracefully around leafy English parkland in spring sunshine. If your top hat happens to be silk, quite rare these days, that is a real bonus. Polly's top hat was specially made for her by hat makers, Pateys.

With the dawn of Saturday, the atmosphere is very different. There is a metallic sense of urgency. The ultimate challenge of the cross-country phase takes centre stage, and the magnificent Gloucestershire estate becomes an amphitheatre of action, spectacle and drama. Those elegant riders are now kitted out in bulky body protectors and crash hats. The horses wear protective tendon boots. Thick grease is spread down all four legs to help them slide over a fence if they should get too close, and they will have a complete change of tack. This could include a jumping saddle designed with a forward seat, a martingale and breastplate – the latter to keep the saddle from sliding backwards – a different bridle and maybe a stronger bit for control. Grooms will have screwed anti-slip studs into the metal horse shoes; how many and how big, will depend on the going.

There are 250,000 spectators on cross-country day. Every fence will be seething with people, several rows deep and craning for a view. It is noisy with warning whistles piercing the air, punctuated by thudding hooves as horses approach, followed by rounds of applause and cheers as they gallop away. There are stewards in tweed jackets and bowler hats mounted on quality hunters, Pony Club runners, loudspeakers giving a non-stop commentary, two or three judges at every fence, children and dogs in the crowd, ambulances which include paramedics, and equine ambulances, spaced around the course, refreshment tents and wine bars, fence repair teams, officials and VIPs travelling in Range Rovers in designated areas. There are packed stands at many fences, and particularly at the Lake Fence. This area becomes a great sea of faces where thousands will gather. They will not be disappointed; there is always at least one dunking, with an unfortunate rider emerging soaked and dripping with cold water.

The Lake Fence is one of the most influential at Badminton, and it was no different that year. Polly must have walked this fence so many times, looking at every possible route and angle. There was the slower circuitous route, and the quicker more difficult option, the latter a one stride combination through to a bounce of upright, beefy rails straight into the lake. If Bumble was going well, this was the way Polly planned to go. Approaching the lake, with its choice of routes, presented a maze of timber. They were painted dazzling white and glinted in the sunshine. Launching themselves into an unknown expanse of rippling water is a leap of faith and obedience for horses. They do not know how deep or wide it is. They have to have complete trust in their jockeys.

Badminton 1989 is another age, and there has been much change, except for one element. It has a magnetism which reaches out to all who compete there. There is a sense of greatness and of history. The fences are notoriously daunting and in those days, with the four-phase speed and endurance, it was a significant test of stamina too. I hoped to witness Polly and Bumble complete the cross-country well. This alone would be a lifetime achievement. I hoped it would be without jumping penalties. This was the absolute intention and the expectation. Bumble had rarely let us down – but was it a dream?

As I write now, in 2014, I had not been to Badminton for a few years. I was finding watching the cross-country rather tedious. Too many competitors completed clear within the time. It was increasingly difficult to justify the challenge of the great event to my golfing husband, who quite correctly observed most of the top results depended predominately on the dressage phase. But this time, I gazed at the fences transfixed. These were huge, imposing and artistically imaginative, designed by Giuseppe Della Chiesa from Italy. In writing this book, I wanted to go again to soak up some of that magic. To take in the deer park, the towering trees, the resplendent yellow-stoned pile that is Badminton House; horses quietly being exercised in those lush, green acres, the world's premier riders going through their paces, the soaring flags of many nations; the vast acres of the tented shopping village, where in 1989 you could buy anything from a diamond ring from Garrards the Crown jewellers, to a silk scarf from Hermes, Pimms in a tall glass to a burger in a bun. I needed to remember how I felt that day, nearly twenty-five years ago.

In 1973, when Lucinda Prior-Palmer won Badminton for the first time, she was only nineteen years old. She attributes most of this success to her horse, Be Fair. However, as she was to reach the top spot another five times, making it six in all, on six different horses, she surely is being extremely modest. My family still thumb through her book *Up, Up and Away* about her horse, Be Fair, and that first Badminton win. There were other notable Badminton winners during that era. Mark Phillips, Richard Meade, Jane Holderness-Roddam among them. With the 1980s others joined them. Mark Todd, Ginny Holgate – later Leng – Mary King and Ian Stark. But for me the most inspirational was Lucinda, and I attribute that to her cross-country riding. How else could she have galvanised a relatively ordinary, but clearly genuine, horse like Killaire to devour a track like Badminton?

Changes have taken place, but it is interesting to compare. The allowed dimensions of the fences and the distance of the cross-country remains virtually unchanged. Many horses finished tired in

2014. Inevitably one asks, were the horses as fit as they should be? From hunting roots Britain used to lead the way when it came to cross-country riding, but other countries, particularly Germany, have learnt how to do it as well as us, which has necessitated increasingly innovative and technical fence design. Many fences are now grouped together, requiring several turns. This involves greater precision, but it must seem less natural for the horse. They gallop in straight lines in the wild. Is this a better scenario or not? Probably yes for spectators and for television, but perhaps not for the horses. Whichever view one takes, this is clearly the future for cross-country courses.

But I have digressed. Back to Badminton 1989, and Wednesday's inspection by the Ground Jury. An occasion in itself, that year was no different. Held opposite the north front of Badminton House which overlooks the lake in the distance, spectators gather early, and jostle and squeeze for a good view. As the time arrives for the 'trot up', not far away in the wings the sound of many hooves can be heard scrunching on gravel. It is like being behind the scenes for a Royal Command performance, and seeing the stars close up. Members of the Ground Jury assemble, stewards stand by and tension builds. There is an audible chatter as crowds, several rows deep, check their programmes and compare notes. In 1989 the judges were Germany's Dr. Springorum, Captain the Hon. Patrick Conolly-Carew from Ireland, and Great Britain's former Olympian, Richard Meade. Heading the Appeal Committee was Vicomte Jurien de la Graviere from France.

We knew Highland Road was in peak form, and I was excited rather than nervous. As Polly led him forward towards the panel of judges, there was a noticeable lustre to his golden coat, and along the muscled crest of his neck, boot-black plaits were dotted in perfect precision. He stood with his head high, and away he trotted, each hoof pinging off the ground, and flicking forward from a lean and taut frame. The sound of steel rang out on the hard surface, even and true like a metronome. All was in order. But there was something else about him – something intangible. He had an aura, a certain assurance. The curtain was raised, a cast of stars was ready, and the first act had begun – while we, the supporters and spectators, looked forward with a mounting sense of excitement, and for me, some trepidation.

Once more our loyal band of supporters had rallied together, and all joined Christopher, Tory and me at the Duke of Beaufort's estate. These included friends, sponsors and family members, my sister Lois, nephews and nieces Mark, Annabel, Juliet, Simon and Charles, and the matriarch, my eighty-one year old mother Grace. They were in cheery mood, and enjoying the experience of being a part of the Highland Road/Polly support team.

Several days before travelling to Badminton from North Wales, I had been in a fever of activity. Horses left behind had to be cared for. There were owners' and sponsors' official passes to be applied for. Hotels were booked and meeting places arranged. Timetables planned for the week away. What clothes to take? Competitors and owners were traditionally invited to a cocktail party at Badminton House the evening before the competition. Queues of traffic, nose to tail, would snake for miles down the approaching country lanes. It was important I had all details in order beforehand. I knew that I would be totally preoccupied once the competition started.

In the days when the cross-country was part of the four phase speed and endurance, organization became a military operation. Highland Road resembled a racehorse in his body mass for Badminton 1989. The total distance he was to cover was nearly sixteen miles. This included the four mile cross-country course, and a two mile gallop round a steeplechase course of nine fences, and around nine miles of trotting through the park. He would be under saddle for a total of eighty-one minutes, with a ten minute break in between, before starting the cross-country challenge of thirty-one fences. Added to that eleven and a half stone was the compulsory weight carried in those days. Polly weighed under nine stone, so Bumble had to carry an extra two and a half stone of dead weight in the form of lead in a weight cloth. Polly had him super, super fit. Timing was crucial in every phase, and arriving at the steeplechase – Phase B – the starter was ready to count you down. A team of people were required in the ten minute box, along with a trunk of spare emergency kit which included a full set of horse shoes and tack. If it was hot, gallons of water were needed, if it was cold, extra rugs for the horse. Vets and blacksmiths waited in readiness. Crowds stood on tiptoe, pressing against the wooden palings of the ten minute box, observing the horses and riders coming and going, and the expertise of the teams preparing them for the cross-country, and caring for the horses returning, possibly dehydrated if the weather was hot and humid.

Having watched Bumble and Polly belt round the steeplechase course, rather too fast as it happens, sixteen seconds inside the optimum, Christopher, Tory and I sped back in the car to the ten minute box. We weaved our way between heaving masses, oblivious to our urgency, our owner's car pass stuck prominently on the windscreen. Then we waited, and Bumble trotted into view through the deer park at the end of Phase C. Intense action followed and there was little time to think from then on, but I had already made my plans. I knew I would be unable to watch or listen once Polly set off. I had parked the car in the competitors' car park situated right by the end of the course. There inside the car I would wait, hoping and praying that I would see Bumble gallop triumphantly through the finish, with my daughter on his back.

It was a strange sensation, sitting in my cocoon with thousands of people amassed all around the vast estate, with the blare of the tannoy, the warning whistles from the stewards, the hundreds of people watching the big screen in the fast food area, and the British Horse Society marquee packed with members. All these people would be watching and listening to the drama unfolding on the cross-country course. Pushing in the tape, I settled into the driver's seat, and waited for Beethoven's fifth piano concerto, *The Emperor*, my eyes fixed on the spot beneath the arch through which the horses completed. I had planned to play the third movement with the power of the orchestra, and the piano galloping at full throttle promising triumph; but instead out came the slow, melodious tones of the second movement. As the music swung effortlessly and serenely, there in my mind was a picture of horse and rider floating from fence to fence. They were as the music, in perfect harmony, in perfect rhythm, possessed just for those twelve minutes of some higher power, transporting them from fence to fence without so much as a hiccup.

Suddenly a jolt, and I sat up. I had lost sense of time, and there in front of me was rider number forty-nine, Sue Benson, galloping through the finish. Polly was number fifty; in a few minutes she should be here, and I felt my heart hitting my ribs. Then, in a blink, hard on the heels of Sue Benson, whipping past my windscreen in a streak of golden dun and blue, came Bumble and Polly. I will never forget that sight. I knew then, I knew, I knew, they had done it. They had got round that mountainous course. At that speed I was certain they had gone well, but I still did not know. However, the rest of the Lyon support gang knew exactly. They had watched every epic jump on the closed circuit. Jubilation is the only word. Memories come flooding back. I have to stop for a minute. I am listening once more to the blessed tones of Beethoven's fifth piano concerto, sublime music that saw me through a lifetime of twelve minutes.

Polly and Bumble's spectacular clear round, and they had gone the quick way through the Lake Fence, was one of the fastest of the day. There had been several problems spread across the course at different fences, and many horses did not complete. Bumble was as fit as a fiddle for the show jumping on Sunday. Thousands filled the great stands around the arena. There was not a spare seat to be seen. Below were the brightly coloured jumps, beautifully presented and bedecked with flowers either side, the grass smooth as baize. The band of Her Majesty's Royal Marines, white helmets shimmering in the sun, would lead the parade. Waiting patiently, attached to the event sponsor's Whitbread drays, the mighty Shire horses stood solid as rock, white feather cascading around their enormous feet, all matching dapple greys.

The mounted competitors would follow. It was all hugely exciting. Christopher and I waited beside Bumble for his turn. The horse stood motionless, gazing into the arena. His dark eyes were wide and shining, his nostrils quivered, and his muzzle curled up, showing his teeth. We listened to the rousing beat of the band, the chink of brass and creak of leather of the Shire horse's gleaming harness, and the thousands of excited voices in the stands. I felt privileged to be a part of it all.

Ginny Leng was the winner that year with Master Craftsman. As the youngest competitor amongst the prize winners, Polly and Bumble were short-listed for the European Championships to be held at Burghley later that year. With her were Ginny Leng, Ian Stark, Rodney Powell, Lorna Clarke and Karen Straker. Highland Road had taken a fifteen year old girl from second place at the Pony Club Championships to four European Gold medals and a National title. A top ten placing at Badminton and selection for the Senior British squad, and Polly was just twenty. Chairperson for the Senior selection panel at that time was Henrietta Knight, later to be the trainer of triple Cheltenham Gold Cup winner, Best Mate.

For me, the experience of Badminton is the zenith. I could not watch the real thing at the time, but later I saw the BBC recording and I can see Bumble now, galloping his heart out along that final stretch past Badminton House, Polly crouching low over the saddle urging him on. He knew he was nearly home. It was twenty-five years ago, but the image of that gallant horse, ears pricked, head stretched out, still brings tears to my eyes.

The Whitebread drays, Bernie Tidmarsh in foreground.

Badminton was the glory – but not long after that epic experience, came the abyss that was Burghley.

In August, along with the other short-listed riders, Bumble and Polly completed Gatcombe as part of the build-up to the Championships. Once more he had to carry extra lead weight, and where Badminton is flat, Gatcombe is hilly. The going was hard that year, and although he went well, Polly did not feel he had quite the same edge that he had shown at Badminton. But there was little time for pondering. Training sessions ensued and Burghley duly arrived. Polly was given her Senior British flag to wear on her jacket, which she is entitled to wear forever.

Built for Sir William Cecil, the first Lord Burghley, as a gift from Queen Elizabeth I in recognition of loyal service, Burghley House is magnificent and a classic example of Elizabethan architecture within Lancelot 'Capability' Brown parkland, which dominates the landscape of the three day event held there every September. The house is open to spectators during the event, and we duly attended the cocktail party on Wednesday evening.

Perhaps it was the demands of a second four star event, just four months after Badminton, which proved too much. Bumble had given his all at Badminton. There is no compulsory weight carried today, and the less demanding short format came into operation after 1989. I believe humping extra lead over the gruelling four phase speed and endurance, particularly the steeplechase, had stretched him to a limit. The undulations at Burghley are notoriously testing. Bumble reached fence twenty-two and then Polly pulled him up. She knew it was over, Bumble could go no further. It was a sad day, and the disappointment was overwhelming.

Bumble was found to have a slight cough after Burghley, but I had already made a decision that I have sometimes questioned. When Highland Road arrived at our farm house in the Welsh hills, a smart horse, not especially big and quite butty, he was eye-catching when fit, but few believed he could reach the heights he did. Today, without the restrictions mentioned earlier, it could have been a different story. He had surpassed all expectations, but now I felt a home with a Junior or Young Rider should be his future. It was a calculated decision without sentimentality. Time mellows and I could not do it today, but at that time ambition overrode any other emotion. Today, I am more patient, I would have given him another chance, with some one day events and perhaps a three star. However, the bottom line was we could not afford to. Bumble was eleven years old, a valuable horse with a hugely impressive record. I knew we must sell him. It must have been a wrenching blow to Polly, but to her credit she never openly questioned the decision.

But Bumble's guardian angel was always there at his shoulder plus that lucky star of destiny. A page in his life was about to be turned. Where would it take him? An advertisement was placed in *Horse and Hound*. It was large and bold. Many phone calls ensued but two were significant. The first was from Germany for a Young Rider, and then one from Italy. Things could have gone either way. The German people are known for their efficiency and I listened to a clipped voice down the phone. It was the German Young Rider team trainer.

'Ja ja vee agree all terms, but first vee must have many examinations and radiographs from unc (our) veterinary.'

Bumble was the soundest horse ever. I did not envisage a problem.

Soon after, a call came from someone whose name I knew in the dealing of International event horses. Jurg Zindell was from Switzerland, and acted as agent in particular to the Italians.

'I have a client from Italy, Count Borromeo. He wishes to purchase your horse for his daughter, Laura. She has followed Highland Road's career, and she wants to ride in the Italian Junior team.'

'What about vetting?' I said.

'Yes, yes – no problem,' Jurg replied. 'We only want the two forefeet X-rayed.'

I replaced the phone and thought about it. The Italians were clearly happy to get on with things, and accept Jurg's recommendations. The German's requirements, however, sounded complicated. They wanted their own vet from Germany, plus multiple X-rays of every joint, of every leg, at every angle. I rang Jurg back and queried him hard on his client. He reassured me. I then insisted on one condition. I must have a written promise from Count Borromeo that Highland Road would be returned to us, on his retirement from eventing. I knew I owed it to him. He must end his days with us at home. This was agreed.

For Bumble, his new life in Italy was the right decision. He went on to have a successful career with Laura, and represented Italy in the

Junior European Championships. Not only did Bumble come back to us, but the Borromeo family are now amongst Polly's closest and most loyal friends, and she has made many visits to Count and Countess Borromeo's home in Italy. Every cloud has a silver lining, and yes, like Dorothy Mackenzie all those years ago, Laura's wish came true too!

Water Jump – Badminton

TEN

FOLLY'S STORY

'No, Tuffy, it's that one I want,' I said, staring at the bright chestnut horse she was sitting on. 'No contest.'

We were at a meet of the Flint and Denbigh hounds gathered outside the Kinmel Arms, near St. Asaph, North Wales. Tuffy Tilly always turned her horses out well, and this horse was gleaming and plaited up. Tall – 16.2 hands high but compact, he was a thoroughbred with a fine-boned head. He was stunning – an eyeful. Tuffy had not had him long and was not planning to sell him just yet. She had already shown me a smart horse, also chestnut, by Carnival Night, a popular stallion standing in Ireland. She was keen for me to have this one and Tuffy is very persuasive. But when my eye alighted on Folly's Last there were no doubts – I wanted this one.

It was 1988. Folly was six years old and inexperienced and I decided to leave him with Tuffy to continue his education. A former eventing International, Tuffy was an expert at producing young horses. Polly, now based at Tetbury, was immersed in her campaign for selection for the British Young Rider team with Highland Road. Aiming for a team place is pressurised and the mindset is competitive and focused. A sensitive and rather indecisive character, Folly needed patience and coaxing. I travelled to Tuffy's yard several times a week to help build gymnastic fences in the manege, where he learnt the intricacies of strides, bounces and corners, or we would box up and take him cross-country schooling. Although talented he was not noticeably brave at the beginning. Loading him into the trailer, he dithered on the ramp, snorting as it wobbled beneath him. The air exploded behind me.

'Oh for pity's sake get *in*, Folly, and stop being a prat,' bellowed Tuffy, waving her arms.

Folly cantered up the ramp, dragging me behind him.

Soon Folly was ready for his first event. I had full trust in Tuffy, and was aware that although Folly was cautious, and liked to be sure where he was putting his feet, he was one hundred percent genuine. He was agile and light-footed, and when he jumped, those feet had springs inside them. I knew that Tuffy could teach him to believe in himself during those formative years, and confidence would come. Faced with a tricky drop fence, Folly nearly ground to a standstill.

He's going to stop, I thought.

But no, Tuffy sat quiet, no panic, a nudge with the heels, he stretched out his neck and popped over.

Sometimes the most talented horses are not the most biddable, they can be tricky, awkward or just plain lazy. 'It's got attitude,' you will often hear. On the other hand, some horses with less ability will always try their utmost to please. If I had to choose, I would rather have the latter. With Folly we were fortunate to have a horse with an abundance of both talent and generosity. He was an absolute Christian.

With Folly's early education at the Tuffy academy complete, Polly took up the reins, and as she was still eligible for the Young Rider squad after Burghley, Christopher Schofield quickly reclaimed her. By the spring of 1990, just seven months after Bumble had left for Italy, she and Folly were invited to Bramham to contest the Young Rider National Championships, and aim for a place on the British squad once again.

It was now clear that further sponsorship would be needed to maintain the horses at the level Polly was competing at. She was awaiting the prize-giving at an event near Ascot sponsored by the Australian transit company TNT International. The managing director of this company was Neil Hansford, who was presenting the prizes. Neil had an interest in horses – he had several on the race track in Australia. With him that day was his ten year old daughter, Lara. As Polly went to receive her prize, Lara tugged at her father's sleeve.

'That's Polly Lyon, she's won four gold medals.'

Polly, always quick to spot an opportunity, soon had Neil engaged in conversation, and with urging on by Lara, a three year sponsorship for a substantial amount of money was agreed. The first public appearance, under the new joint sponsorship of TNT International and Samuel Banner & Company, was at Windsor Horse Trials in May with Buckspinner, followed in June with Folly's Last in the Young Rider National Championships at Bramham.

Neil wanted the full works for publicity for his company. Smart competition rugs arrived for each horse, black with red braid and the company logo stitched crimson on white across the corner. Polly and grooms, which included me, were given jackets with the logo emblazoned across the back. The *pièce de résistance* was a gigantic horse box in TNT colours – orange and white. Inside were partitions to carry five horses with living for us at the front. Splashed along one side was written TNT INTERNATIONAL – PROUD SPONSORS OF POLLY LYON.

Galloping across the other side were images of horses; red, white and black. It was, as Neil intended, a visual showstopper to be seen swishing up the motorways, and rolling up to prestigious events like Windsor, Badminton and Blenheim.

With the arrival of a new horse box, I decided I should assist Polly with the driving by passing the HGV test – Heavy Goods Vehicle – which Polly had already achieved. I booked myself in for the intensive six months training course in Gloucester. My instructor was Frank. He was ex-army and had trained soldiers to drive trucks and tanks. Strictly authoritarian, he did, though, have his little quips. Heaven help you if you failed to use the wing mirrors or left a nervous foot hovering over the clutch pedal. We climbed up into the cab, and set off down the busy dual carriageway towards the city. My eyes fixed ahead, and grasping the steering wheel as we bowled along, it was just minutes before a heavy boot shoved my foot angrily off the clutch pedal, and a West Country voice bellowed down my left ear, 'Yorr wing mirrors, what about yorr bl--dy wing mirrors. Now turrn those priddy oiys this way and use yorr flaming wing mirrors!'

Neil Hansford was a roly-poly ebullient Aussie with a razor sharp wit. We were at an event near Savernake in Wiltshire. It was hot and the air hung heavy and humid. The horses waited sleepily, and Polly and I trudged round the hilly cross-country course, when the heavens opened and thunder rumbled. Dashing to the horse box we piled into the living area along with Neil, Lara and a wet dog. The rain rattled on the roof like a shower of pebbles, while we waited in the clammy fug of the Luton. Polly set off to show jump her first horse. She returned rather pink in the face, settled the horse, climbed into the Luton, plonked herself down and threw off her jacket. Not a great one for the English weather, Neil had closeted himself inside the box with a bottle of wine.

'I'm absolutely cooked,' puffed Polly, pulling off her tight crash hat, steam rising from it like a lathered horse, wet hair clinging in dark strands to her forehead.

She placed the hat on the table, and Neil reached out and picked it up. Peering inside, he sniffed, and chortling into his glass gurgled. 'Hey Parlley, this ole hat pongs like a sumo wrestler's jarck strap!'

Windsor drew near and things were not going to plan. Buckspinner started to cough and two days before Windsor we had no choice but to withdraw him. However, all was not lost, as we had complimentary tickets to the member's enclosure and were able to give Neil a good day and introduce him round. There was also Bramham in a fortnight, to showcase our star horse – Folly's Last. The pressure was rising and the usual worries began banging around in my head.

Just before leaving for Bramham, I met Polly for a jumping session with Folly. But as they trotted across the field I stared in dismay as she pulled him up. He did not seem quite level. It was barely noticeable, his legs and feet were cool, and there was no swelling or pulse. Having missed Windsor, to pull out of Bramham would be a disaster for the new sponsors. I dreaded the thought of ringing Neil and giving him the news for the second time.

'We *have* to take him, Polly, even if you only do the dressage. You absolutely must be seen.'

But first of all we had to get him through the veterinary inspection in five day's time.

'Wrap him up in cotton wool, remove his front shoes, poultice his feet, ice tight his legs, just walk him, we are going to have to risk it.'

Bramham Park is one of the most popular events on the eventing calendar. It has a convivial atmosphere and is well patronised by spectators, with trade stands and displays in the side arenas. At the end of the competition, a long-list would be announced for the Young Rider European Championships in September, so from the point of view of those contenders it was a very serious event indeed. The inspection by the Ground Jury took place in front of the house, which was offset by lawns where crowds gathered to watch. There is always a palpable air of anticipation at these inspections, and horses are presented to the three waiting bowler hats – known as the Ground Jury – plaited and polished. Time draws near, the adrenalin is pumping and horses are sharpened up a little. We never had a worry with Highland Road, but here at Bramham with Folly's Last, it would be like watching a cat on hot bricks.

Eventually the steward looked searchingly through the waiting bays, chestnuts, greys and others, and called out, 'Folly's Last, next.'

There was gleaming gold in Folly's chestnut coat that day, and it shimmered in the sun as Polly led him towards the judges. The three looked him over and then waved them on. I held my breath. Polly steadied at the top by a large tub of red geraniums and prepared to turn. Folly jiggled a little, and Polly shortened the rein. He remembered his training and in precise unison they jogged back. Everyone watched – it was quiet, just the sound of four hooves – Folly's hooves.

'Trit trot, trit trot, one two, one two,' – all the way back to the Ground Jury. *Perfect.* The three bowler hats looked at each other and nodded. 'Folly's Last, pass.'

The words blared over the tannoy, and the next horse came forward. Giving nothing away with the expression on her face, Polly led Folly back towards me and we silently went '*Phew.*'

So onward to the dressage on Friday. We had Thursday in between to check for the umpteenth time for any problems. Four challenging days lay ahead. Would that niggle rear its head at the vital horse inspection on the final day?

'Don't trouble trouble, till trouble troubles you.'

My mother's words sat in my head. I knew that Folly was capable of producing an outstanding test. Go for that and take each day as it comes. Only Polly and I knew about the question mark hanging over our horse.

Rain poured down on Wednesday night, and we drove round the roads and tracks slithering and squelching through the mud, while Neil Hansford gamely walked the cross-country course with us. Gill Watson had been greatly instrumental in helping Polly with Folly's Last that spring, and he looked like a star in the making. With the calming influence of Gill, they cantered into the dressage arena with confidence. Sure enough the pair came up with a leading score after two days of dressage.

There are times when, tackling a major competition, you know that your horse is well up to the test and should succeed. Highland Road's biggest challenge had been Badminton, and the challenge turned out to be a triumph. Bramham's cross-country with Folly's Last was a cliff edge. He was inexperienced at this level and I was very nervous indeed. As horse and rider prepared to enter the start box, I walked quickly away and, melting into the crowds, headed towards the car parks. No one noticed as I paced the ground checking my watch. Eventually, I set off back to the thronged ten minute box. I saw the familiar wooden palings that fenced off the start and finish. It was buzzing with action; teams of riders, horses and grooms. Some combinations were sharp and ready to set off, others galloped through the finish relieved and tired. I searched for my horse and jockey. Was that a chestnut horse I could see? Was it Folly?

I began to run. I saw that the chestnut horse was indeed Folly. I felt my face break into a smile, and I ran faster. He was being washed down, and nearby were happy faces, hugs, pats, and people crowding round Polly. They had completed a copy book round and once again a venture had paid off. We celebrated well that evening, but tomorrow was another day. Would Folly be sound for the final challenge, the veterinary trot up and the showjumping? Early next morning we prepared ourselves for a very private inspection of Folly's Last.

There was a sense of quiet activity as we arrived at the lines of stabled horses in the chilly grey dawn, with contented munching of hay, a few clinking buckets and horses whinnying as they waited for a feed. Folly pricked his ears as we approached, and I stroked his nose. Pulling open the bolts we entered the stable, and bending down unravelled the support bandages and felt his legs. They were cool and firm – so far, so good. Quietly we led him off to trot up. This was serious business. Polly was on the brink of becoming Young Rider National Champion for the second time and I felt tense. Folly raised his head and began to trot towards me with Polly alongside. I nodded, relieved. Four even foot falls. We swapped, and this time Polly watched – the same. All was well that early Sunday morning, Folly was A1 for the inspection panel.

With Gill Watson and Christopher Schofield beaming amongst the spectators, Polly and her lovely chestnut horse went on to complete a clear showjumping round followed by a victorious lap of honour. Now Young Rider National Champions once more, the pair had secured their place for the European Championships. In 1990 the host nation was Great Britain, and the event was held at Rotherfield Park, in Hampshire.

The British team selected for the Young Rider Championships that year was William Fox-Pitt with the faithful Steadfast, Lynn Bevan with the smart chestnut Horton Point – this horse would later win Badminton ridden by Mark Todd – Daniel Hughes, a pupil of Ian Stark's with Finneas Fin, and Polly with Folly's Last. It was a strong team but the Germans too had an impressive squad and, for the first time for many years, the Russians, travelling for nearly five days by horse box across Europe, had brought a team. I drove the long, winding journey from North Wales to Hampshire, towing a well-stocked caravan for use as a gathering point for our family and supporters at the Championships. Pulling into Rotherfield Park I arrived a little late for the inspection by the Ground Jury. It had started, and some horses had already been presented. I searched for Polly and saw her waiting beside Folly amongst the melee of riders and horses. Folly appeared fine, looking about with bright eyes. Polly, however, was stony-faced. I sensed something wrong. But it was too late for questions.

'Folly's Last,' called the tannoy. Their turn had come.

Lines of keen spectators watched along the trot up area several rows deep. I spotted Christopher Schofield and the selectors smiling and expectant. Their star competitor was about to be inspected. The three judges waved the pair on, and they trotted away. Folly was well trained, he knew what to do and he trotted back towards the judges obediently. He was a fit horse, ready for a three day event. But oh sugar! I grimaced; something did not look quite right. His stride was pottery. Was it just me or had the judges noticed too? Folly could be ejected from the competition before he had even started. I looked over at Christopher Schofield and Gill Watson. The smiles had vanished. They had noticed too.

'Folly's Last will be inspected again in the holding box.'

I groaned inwardly, but all was not yet lost. Folly was not the only horse awaiting a second look; there were a couple of foreign horses, too. The judges plus the official veterinary surgeon arrived at the holding box. The vet examined Folly and an intense discussion ensued, which included Polly. There were solemn expressions and a lot of nodding, but then everyone relaxed and smiled, and Folly was waved through, as were the other two horses. Torture over, but not quite.

Immediately after this inspection, Christopher Schofield buttonholed us and insisted on a further look at Folly. Medals were at stake. Two reserves waited in the wings. He desperately wanted Polly for the team, but there was a stiff cross-country ahead, and Folly could still run as an individual. Once more the horse was trotted up, this time under the eagle eye of Christopher, Gill and Bob Baskerville. The conclusion was a slightly bruised sole or possibly a corn. Not too serious and Polly was given the nod, but something had to be done and quickly. We had less than forty-eight hours to sort it. Action stations and an SOS to our farrier in Gloucestershire. There was a farrier on site, but we decided our own was the safest bet. Everything hung on Folly's two front feet, and he knew them best.

By the time the blacksmith arrived it was pitch dark, and there were no lights in the temporary stables erected for the event. We had decided to fit leather pads between the front steel shoes and Folly's soles. Our blacksmith would need all the skill he possessed to fit and nail the pads and shoes onto Folly's thin thoroughbred soles by the light of torches. Swiftly he removed the two shoes and prodded and poked about and squeezed with the hoof testers. Polly held her horse and stroked his neck, keeping him still. Two torches held by myself and Polly's head girl, Kate, beamed onto his feet. The blacksmith measured, cut, and fitted the leather pads. He reset the shoes and tapped and hammered in the nails, making sure all was firm. That was it; we had done all we could and we thanked him for coming all that way at night.

'No problem,' he said. 'Especially when I can say I have shod the gold medal winner.'

His optimism cheered me and I wished I could have felt as upbeat. Thursday and Friday dawned fine and hot, and the ground was firming up all the time. Two days of dressage commenced, and predictably Germany went ahead, with a leading score from Peter Mueller. Back at the stables Folly was being prepared and Kate had plaited him. Auburn mane as fine as a maiden's, his plaits neatly sewn along the crest of his neck. Chestnut coat burnished like a conker. Under the dark leather of the saddle was fitted a white saddle cloth, and stitched across this was the Union Jack. Waiting for them by the dressage arenas were our supporters – Neil Hansford, family members – my sister Lois and Oliver Beck, Christopher and Tory, British team members, Christopher Schofield and the selectors, and several contenders from abroad. Gill was giving Polly last minute help, and then their number was called. I looked across and saw what I knew could be a winning combination – if they could just hold it all together for the next ten minutes.

The bell rang and they cantered in. The test had begun. Silence descended. Then slowly, I began to relax. There before me was a display of the grace and star quality that I had first noticed in North Wales. With every movement Folly was a Nureyev. He sprang lightly and obediently from step to step, while Polly hardly moved, concentration total, and the test dazzled. Everyone knew it was good, but what would the three judges in their little boxes think? Well of course they thought it was good, too, very good in fact. Top of the leader board once more, the pair had overtaken Germany's Peter Mueller and that is where they stayed – for the time being. There were still another two days of stiff competition ahead.

Course designer Hugh Thomas's cross-country course was big and testing that year. The track was hilly, and the sun blazed in a humid heat. Fitness would tell. By the end of the day the scores from the dressage were likely to change. This course was going to cause trouble. Sure enough there were falls early on and several refusals. One by one

111

foreign teams clocked up penalties, and there were problems with the home team, too. Polly needed a good clear to keep the British in touch for gold. Those were her instructions as she and Folly galloped out of the start box, and headed towards fence one.

Photos I have of Folly, towards the end of Rotherfield's cross-country course on that sweltering day, show him looking quite tired, his neck dark with sweat. But brave and generous horse that he was, and coaxed on by Polly, they did the business and completed a fast clear round, increasing their own leading position, and keeping the British team in front.

Now it was only the showjumping. As predicted, the cross-country had caused significant trouble. Polly was set to win a Young Rider team and individual gold medal for the second time, and once more she was last to jump. The pressure was intense, but she did have a fence in hand. The best way for you to know the outcome is the bold heading and report splashed across *Horse and Hound* later that week.

ROTHERFIELD PARK AND FOLLY'S LAST GIVE POLLY A RECORD FIRST

Polly Lyon led an invincible home squad to team gold at the Young Rider European Championships. The British challenge for the Young Rider European Championships was so strong that the team of Polly Lyon, William Fox-Pitt, Daniel Hughes and Lynn Bevan took team gold from last year's champions Germany. Polly Lyon became the first Young Rider to also win the individual title for a second time having already won it in 1988 on Highland Road.

For the third time in four years, I listened and watched as the National Anthem rang out, the Union Jack was raised, and Polly stepped forward. Double gold, again. We were riding on an ever increasing tidal wave of success, a magic carpet. It was hard to take in. On the Sunday of Rotherfield, as Folly waited to enter the showjumping arena, Christopher Schofield put his hand on my shoulder and said, 'You are about to make history.'

He had included me in Polly's success, but it was a team and family effort too. I don't know whether anyone has repeated Polly's record, of two Young Rider individual and team gold medals on two different horses, since those days, but I think probably not.

From triumph, to tragedy. The details of what happened next are distressing. However, it is a very long time ago, and part of the story of our life with horses. The intermittent soundness problems we had had with Folly led to a decision to give him several month's lay off. He eventually returned to competition and demonstrated his undoubted ability with a foot perfect round in the Advanced class at the Open Championships at Gatcombe Park. We knew Folly had the class of a four star International horse. We looked forward to the following spring and that winter Polly went on a skiing holiday with friends.

It was about 4pm in January when the phone rang. The voice at the other end was one of Polly's students at Charlton Park, Malmesbury, which was Polly's training base.

'Come quickly. It's Folly. He's down.'

'Has the vet been rung? Where is Kate?' I barked, rushing for the keys of the car.

'Three vets have been contacted. Kate is with him.'

'I am coming immediately. Keep ringing the vet.'

And with that, hunched over the steering wheel with an ominous sense of doom, I sped the three miles from Tetbury to Charlton.

The students met me as I raced up the long Charlton Park drive and to South Park near the house. Stretched out on the grass was the bulk of Folly. The saddle and bridle had been removed, and lay in a heap on the ground beside him. It had been a crisp cold day, but the winter evening was descending and now it was bitter and freezing. He lay heavily on his side and his breathing rasped with shuddering difficulty. He was shivering in spasm. His legs stretched stiff in front of him, his eyes glazed and unseeing. Someone had put a rug over him and also round Kate, who was kneeling by his head, beside herself with grief. She quickly explained that Folly had collapsed with no warning while she had been lungeing him.

I knew immediately that something very serious indeed had happened to Folly. Deep down my instincts told me he had gone from us, and if he survived he would never be the same horse. But these thoughts were quickly pushed away as emergency action took over, while I scanned the drive for the vet, and sent someone back to the stables for more rugs.

There is something utterly heart-rending seeing a powerful and beautiful animal lying helpless and ungainly on the ground. Horses rely on flight in the wild, and know how vulnerable they are without the ability to flee. This is why foals are on their feet within hours of being born. For the next two hours we desperately tried to save Folly. The scene that took place in that field on an icy January night, with the lit up windows of the great mansion house of Charlton appearing to watch the drama unfolding in the park below, was reminiscent of a Shakespearian tragedy. Immediately after my arrival Sven Kold, the vet, bumped his way across the field, jumped out of his car and ran across to Folly. Sven was the Swedish colleague of John Kilingbeck, who was at another call but on his way, too. Within minutes Sven had life-saving treatment under way but light was fading fast; soon it would be too dark to see. An SOS reached the estate workers and with haste, emerging through the gloom like great monsters, rumbled two tractors, headlights blazing. Quickly they beamed onto the horse, and Sven worked on.

Folly was fighting for his life, and his feral instincts told him he must get up. Staggering to his feet he reeled wildly and attempted to run. Syringes, drips and bottles went flying. Half a ton of animal, semi-conscious and out of control, was potentially dangerous, and I grabbed the lunge line from Kate. With a groan Folly buckled, and collapsed to the ground once more. During all this time I had not taken my eyes off the horse or Sven, and time had passed unnoticed. Then I looked up, and in the dim light I made out a semi-circle of people standing quietly. Word had got round and Polly's staff, estate workers, others living in estate cottages and Mickey and Linda – Lord and Lady Suffolk – had all come to support, to offer help in any way they could. They stood silently in that field in the freezing night, watching as Sven worked on. The only sound was the drone of the tractors and the rasping breathing of Folly. Gradually the horse became quiet and still. Life was slipping away. But with one final and pitiful effort, Folly tried to rise again, and then slid to the ground, and I saw dark blood trickle from his ear.

The semi-circle of people who had bravely come to support knew it was over, and they quietly turned and melted into the gloaming in their own sorrow. Linda came over and kindly asked me back to the house, but I needed to see Sven and John Kilingbeck, who had by then arrived. Sven was gathering his equipment as I made my way in the darkness to his car, but I hesitated. Vets witness the death of horses and animals many times, but as I came near I saw that there were tears in Sven's eyes. Close by stood John in silent sadness. He had known Folly well.

A chestnut tree is planted where Folly died in South Park, Charlton. A memory to a horse that was gentle in nature, noble in beauty, courageous in trust. A horse that was perhaps a little fragile, but at his height had shown all the power and grace of the thoroughbred that he was, and who had given us his best years.

It was concluded that Folly had died from an aneurysm.

ELEVEN

POINT-TO-POINTING – TAMOSAGA – DENSTONE WANDERER

Step back to 1989. Polly's debut at Badminton is looming, when ring – ring – ring, the insistent tone of the telephone demanded my attention. It was bound to be one of the girls.

'Hugo has had a rugby injury and is unable to ride in Saturday's point-to-point – he has offered me the ride on his horse Trumpton.'

I listened as the familiar voice at the other end, rattling with excitement, was about to transport us into a new chapter in our life with horses; a very different world – an exhilarating world – the point-to-point scene. It was Tory.

Tory had ridden successfully in Junior eventing team trials, and later at intermediate level, and she was rapier quick when showjumping against the clock, but it was in galloping and jumping between the flags that she found her true forte.

'Oh my God! What's the horse like? Can it jump?' My questions fired fast.

'It will be fine. I've ridden Trumpton loads of times on the gallops.'

Tory worked in banking in London, and Hugo Barker was a good friend. I knew she had been riding out at weekends on Toby Balding's gallops in Hampshire.

'Where is it?' I said, my curiosity and interest by now well fired up, and thinking perhaps Warwickshire or Gloucestershire. Living in North Wales we were used to making long journeys.

'It's in Somerset, on the Devon border.'

Tory riding in a point-to-point was an experience I could not miss, and I quickly began shuffling through the shelves for a map. I made the decision to travel there and back in a day, a round trip of 520 miles.

The first point-to-point took place in Southern Ireland in 1752. It happened as a result of a challenge between two Irishmen to race across country on horseback from one point – the steeple of Buttevant church, to another point – the steeple of St. Mary's church, both in County Cork. National Hunt racing also evolved from this first race hence the name – steeplechasing. At that far off time people raced in their hunting kit on hunters, across natural country – hedges, ditches, and anything that came along. Smart thoroughbreds, jockeys in racing silks with stirrups pulled up short, were to evolve as the sport has become more professional.

Point-to-pointing has a character all of its own. It is patronised by country people, hunt followers, farmers, people who enjoy a punt, racing enthusiasts and families out for a day in the countryside. There is the usual assortment of rural attire, and these days anything goes, although owners, officials and connections with participating horses and jockeys are traditionally well turned out, which includes bowler hats and tweed jackets. One very cold day at Eyton-on-Severn point-to-point, a sleepy hamlet by the river in Shropshire, I spotted a lady wrapped up in a beautiful full length mink coat. It was safe to assume there would be no bunny huggers amongst the assembled enthusiasts.

Invariably reached down winding lanes, with venues in tree-studded countryside, there is an abundance of high class horses, talented jockeys, and competition is feisty and keen. But it also retains a rather delightful, timeless atmosphere away from the rush and crowds of commuter, and consumer Britain. I always enjoy and feel at home at a point-to-point, wherever it takes place. I can take the dogs, too, which means they get an outing as well.

Two days after that phone call, I scrunched up the drive of Pen Parc in the silence of a pink dawn rising over the Welsh mountains, with my terrier Cracker for company. Several hours later I arrived in the hills of the West Country, and pulled into the point-to-point car park. I looked keenly round for Tory; she had already spotted me, and was dashing towards the car – Tory always dashes. With her for moral support came her good friend Emma Knight – now Bird. Hugo hobbled behind on crutches in traditional garb of brown trilby, with binoculars dangling round his neck. 'Trumpton will take good care of Tory,' he assured me, smiling.

I cannot recall watching any of the other races. Emma and I were fully occupied fitting five foot two Tory into six foot two Hugo's green and black racing silks, and lightweight breeches. The month was March and it was cold. The lady's changing tent shuddered in the wind, and with shivering fingers we struggled with the slippery silk sleeves, which flapped round Tory's knees. We rolled them up into a lumpy bunch round her wrists, securing them with tape and elastic bands. The same redesigning was required with the thin white breeches. With the waist reaching up to her armpits and nearly over her head, we got busy with safety pins, and more tape round her middle. In future years Tory stood out as a trim little figure in her racing colours – sky blue with black stars – striding purposefully into the ring, and slapping her boot with her whip. However, on this occasion, any thoughts of catching the eye as an attractive lady jockey was off the agenda. Here at the Cotley point-to-point Tory was trussed up like a Christmas turkey. But this mattered not a jot, once the starter's flag went down.

As the time of the race drew near, the jitters became evident, and with Tory finally sorted in Hugo's kit she then announced she wanted a pee. Once more Emma and I got busy, and the breeches were again redesigned and resecured. Then there came the crash hat. Placing Hugo's white silk on top it wafted down over her eyes like a billowing parachute.

She has got to be able to see, I thought in a panic, and shoving up the silk I pulled the ties at the front as tight as I could, when *ping*, they snapped. More safety pins and elastic bands, and the clock ticked by. This pantomime was fast becoming a comedy act, rather than preparation for a race on a galloping thoroughbred, and Emma and I were by now giggling helplessly, and with nerves.

Tory was legged up onto the trusty Trumpton, who was a good jumper but maybe not the fastest, and away they cantered to the start. Surprisingly, I watched the whole of the race, without covering my eyes at every fence. In what was to become customary fashion, Tory started in the middle, and then resolutely picked her way through the field and finished a good third. 'God he jumped like a stag,' announced a flushed Tory, bending double over her lead-laden saddle and humping it over to the scales. We had all had a lot of fun, and as I drove the long way back to Wales, with Cracker curled up on the passenger seat beside me, I had plenty of time to ponder the possibility of more entertainment on the point-to-point circuit. But I had no inkling then how gripped I would become with this new equestrian sport. With one daughter competing in her first point-to-point, and another tackling Badminton for the first time, it was a high-octane twelve days and I probably lost a few pounds, and certainly some sleep.

The following week Tory was offered another ride on an enormously tall chestnut horse, somewhat resembling a camel, and this time she won. The bug had bitten, and getting a few chance rides was never going to tick the box for Tory.

Soon another phone call ensued.

'Seamus Mullins has seen a horse which he says would be a really good buy for me to race.'

Amateur jockey to Toby Balding, Seamus – now a professional trainer – also had his own yard in Appleshaw near Andover, where he trained point-to-pointers. He and Tory had decided to purchase a right little character called Tamosaga, he to train and she to race. Extremely well-bred by the American stallion Seaepic out of Tamoretta, at eleven years of age Tamosaga was easing off the top of his game.

Tamosaga was naughty! Not for nothing was his stable name Tinker. When the vet came to examine him for purchase, and got on to ride (as they often did in those days), Tamosaga promptly dropped his shoulder, and deposited him on the ground. He had a prominent white blaze down his dark bay face and two white stockings, so he had just a look of the gypsy horse about him. He possessed a keen sense of humour, and frequently ejected his jockey out on exercise. Peering down at the unfortunate rider he then refused to allow them back on board. Hacking him out on his own was chancy. Many a time I followed Tinker, cracking a lunge whip as close as possible to his swaggering rear end, while with a wicked eye he threatened to about turn, and take himself and his rider off home.

Once on the race track, however, he was a proper professional, a reliable jumper, competitive and gutsy. He did, though, have another little trick. Waiting at the start he would only turn one way, so Tory had to think quickly and outwit him when the flag went down, otherwise she could find herself facing backwards and returning to the horse box park.

Tory's account of lady jockeys gathering at the start of a ladies' race, compared to mixed races, was described thus.

'There was a lot of jostling for position with panicky calls to the starter.'

'Wait, wait sir, my girth needs tightening.'

'Wait, wait sir, I'm not ready.'

'Wait, wait sir, I'm just making another turn.'

But that apart, the shared element of danger, along with battling through rain and sleet, with wind whipping across your face, creates a strong bond and camaraderie between the jockeys.

Tinker's first point-to-point took place at Tweseldown racecourse, and he was our introduction to racehorse ownership, providing us with the fun of participation. Tweseldown racecourse, in Fleet, Hampshire, evolved in the 19th century. It closed as a racecourse in 2013, but still holds several equestrian-linked events. The site was originally purchased in 1854 by the British army for troop training for the Crimean War. Queen Victoria came to visit in 1886, where she took the salute for 15,000 soldiers. Ten years later in 1896 it was officially opened as a National Hunt racecourse, and the 19th century buildings, which include a grandstand with clock face, and jockey's weighing room, are listed. They still have much appeal, with wooden arches enclosing a low level veranda, red tiled roofs, and outside, a life-size bronze of a course-winning horse and jockey. Well worth taking a little time to look at. The equestrian events at the 1948 London Olympics were held at Tweseldown.

The control tower, set high on a hillock, is in contrast to the main buildings. It is tall, stark and rather ugly, with glass windows all round at the top. Viewing from there must have been good, because as spectators, trying to watch a race at Tweseldown was pretty hopeless. The area is heavily wooded and the track weaved in and out between silver birch trees, scrubby bushes and purple heather. The horses appeared and disappeared before you could say Jack Rabbit. As the horses left the paddock everyone rushed to watch, scrabbling up the stone steps to the top of the hill by the Control Tower. A large crowd congregated and, standing on tiptoe, peering round spectators, running from one side of the tower to the other, you hoped to catch a glimpse of your horse and jockey.

It was a cold day in February 1990, and inside the building a fire blazed, the logs spitting and sparking, the heat enveloping us as we stepped from the biting wind outside into the warmth of the crowded room. White-clothed trestles were piled high with home-made refreshments, and smiling ladies served hot pies, sandwiches and chocolate cake topped with thick icing. The large wooden fireplace, also late 19th century, along with the wooden panelling, added to the individual character of the place. These were just small things, but all contributed to the enjoyment of that particular day for me, because it would be the first time I witnessed a horse of ours win a race. With the winning post positioned just below the control tower, I watched with amazement as Tory and Tamosaga swept through ahead of the field. There is nothing like the exhilaration of winning for the first time. It was totally unexpected and the excitement I can recall so well. I ran down the steps from the control tower to welcome them in.

Point-to-pointing, noticeably in the south, does have a significant element of well-heeled supporters from the upper end of the British social strata. A good chunk will primarily be there for the party from the rear of the Range Rover. In the 1990s green wellies, Barbours, tweed jackets and brown felt trilbies mingled predominately amongst the hundreds of people who live and work in the countryside; farmers, farriers, grooms, vets, hunt servants etc. There are also plenty of dogs – Jack Russell terriers, spaniels, labradors, other terriers. There are not many designer-clipped poodles, chihuahuas, and Afghans, as in dogs, though. It still amuses me when watching the recording of this race at Tweseldown to pick up a girl's voice coming through the babble of sound.

'Oh, look I say. It's Taramasalata.'

And there below me, zipping past the winning post, in top spot, was our Tamosaga.

From Seamus Mullins, the following season Tamosaga went to trainer Dick Baimbridge. Dick's name is iconic in point-to-point racing. He is a farmer alongside training horses, and is based in the Berkeley Hunt country on the River Severn in Gloucestershire. In 2012 he celebrated training 500 winners on the amateur circuit as well as many others in Hunter Chases. Christopher and I made several trips to the aptly named Hill Farm to watch Tory ride out with the string through the park, and then gallop up the steep hills on the farm. The horses blew hard and worked hard. When asked what his secret to success was, Dick maintained that routine and discipline for the horses was essential. I noticed this when being shown round the stables. There was no nonsense, and the horses clearly had great respect for him. Dick's horses were always supremely fit. He did not have gallops, but the park at Berkeley Castle and several trips up and down the hills did the job. In his autobiography, champion trainer Paul Nicholls attributes much of his great success to his early apprenticeship spent with Dick Baimbridge.

Tory and Tinker completed two Hunter Chases as well as several more point-to-points. The first Hunter Chase was at Bangor-on-Dee and the second at Lingfield. There, from a large field, the winner that day was Robert Alner, with Tory second. What a fine one to follow as runner-up. Bangor-on-Dee turned out to be smugly satisfying for us. Racing at your local course is a bit more pressurised because there will be people there that know you, whereas if all goes awry further away, you can sort of anonymously melt off into the background. On the 1st February 1991 it was cold and wet, wet, wet. Well-known race goers, like the Griffith family from Denbigh, and the Barlows from Tarporley, had horses running, and although successful in the eventing world – Polly had already won three European titles – we were comparative novices here. However, both Dick and his champion jockey, Alison Dare, had travelled up with Tamosaga, and this would not have gone unnoticed by the rest of the field.

Christopher, Dick and I waited in the paddock, hunched into our coats, Christopher puffing on a cigarette, while the rain trickled down our necks. Alison was leading a jaunty Tamosaga round, and eventually out came several lean and battle-hungry male jockeys. I quickly looked for Tory, and emerging from the ladies' changing room appeared just one small girl in her light blue silks and black stars. Someone did once say to me the colour mix was interesting – black and blue, and seeing stars. This all seemed quite bizarre, and I rather wondered what we were doing there, but there was no time for nail biting. The bell rang. The rug was whipped off Tamosaga, a leg up from Dick, and cantering off to the start with the lads, the pair disappeared into the swirling mist.

The sight of Dick Baimbridge, a long way from his patch in Gloucestershire, must have worried some because, as I was later to discover, while the jockeys were circling at the start, one or two attempted to unnerve Tory, exhibiting a total lack of couth to the lady jockey in their midst, muttering expletives like – 'f…ing lady jockeys. Bl..dy nuisance getting in the way' etc. etc.

I must hasten to add that Tory's former Pony Club team member, James Griffith, was not one of them. Always such a decent young man, so tragically losing his life in a motor accident, he wished her a good ride.

As usual, rather than wait amongst the crowd, I made my way towards the final fence and leant on the rails to watch the race. I couldn't see the start, but heard the commentator.

'They have set off at a tremendous pace with Tamosaga up with the leaders.'

Then the troubles began. A horse dug his heels in and refused at the second. Despite the mud the pace was relentless, and several horrible jumps followed, which included one by Tinker, dropping him back to midfield. Completing the first circuit Chris Stockton took up the lead aboard Busted Spring, and straining my eyes I noticed Tinker was struggling in the sticky going, and had drifted further back. Then, oh sugar! He skews badly over the birch and loses ground again.

Game's up, I thought, as Tory lurched towards his ears but miraculously forced herself back in the plate.

The weather worsened, and horses were visibly tiring and losing heart. But, unlike the others, Tinker was getting a second wind, and forging on. As they swung towards home, he creeps up the field, and I lean forward, grasping the rails. There are now only five horses left in contention with three fences to jump. The rest of the field are knackered. They disappear in the blanket of rain, but I hear the commentator.

'Nightsafe has pulled up. Ah Hello has pulled up. And you can forget about Busted Spring, Oakley House, and Frenchman's Fancy.'

I search the horizon, and Tinker's still there. I can make out his sheepskin nose-band, but as he gets closer his big white blaze has disappeared; it is completely obliterated by mud stuck to his face like glue. He has inched back to third, and the penultimate fence is looming.

Can he hold that place? Will he even finish? Questions jump about in my head. I watch him straddle the final fence, and meander across the track. Tory glances quickly behind. A horse comes up to challenge on the run in. Determined to keep her place, she urges Tinker on, and with heads down the pair dig in. By now I am running along the white rails, and three horses gallop past me. Staring as they cross the finish, I notice the winner is Mountain Crash, who has led for most of the way, but Tinker has stayed on to finish third, and Tory pats him gratefully on the neck. I ran to meet them as they turned back towards the paddock.

Watching Tamosaga battling bravely to hold his place and Tory never giving up, while the rest of the field had either ground to a halt or staggered in a long way behind, was gripping and immensely satisfying.

Yes, I thought later. *Those aforementioned jockeys, at the start, had underestimated Tory's tenacity and Tinker's ability to stay.*

After two seasons Tamosaga left us, and went on to give experience to a first season lady jockey.

In 1992 a handsome grey horse called Denstone Wanderer – stable name Stony – joined our family. He was a large pebble-grey horse with bright white dapples dotted over his perfect frame, a fine head and sleek legs. He stood around 16.3 hands high, and was not without ability. A kind horse, he was, however, idle. But once he arrived at Dick Baimbridge's yard he had to change his ways. Stony's first race with us was at Badbury Rings in Dorset. At the end of that season, write ups on Denstone Wanderer went something like this:

Denstone Wanderer, prone to being tailed off. Appreciates forcing tactics. However, since moving to Dick Baimbridge's yard he has been transformed.

Tory's description of riding horses trained by Dick echoes this write-up. 'They felt different,' she said. 'They had a purpose.' Not only did Dick get them physically fit, but mentally too. They were out there to do a job, and they knew it. One day, Tory was at Dick's, galloping with the string. The horse Dick was riding appeared to be doing nothing wrong, but clearly what could be seen and what he could feel going on underneath him were very different. All of a sudden there was an audible, and severe, reprimand. The effect on the horse was instant. Galvanized into action, the offending animal grabbed the bit, leapt forward several gears, and left the string trailing.

And so, on we go to Badbury Rings. The first race with a new horse is an exciting unknown. There were plenty of supporters there that day, notably the Knight family out in force – parents, boyfriends and sisters. Tory's particular minder, Emma Knight, was clucking round as she had generously done the first time with Trumpton. But we were rather more seasoned race participants by now, and Tory was noticeably composed. The bookies had Stony as favourite, so there was a silent confidence but coupled with the pressure of expectation, and word would have circulated that this horse was now trained by Dick.

The bookies may have been flashing Denstone Wanderer's name as the likely winner, but there were some tight-faced competitors, and the race would be fiercely fought. Off they set and, passing Cracker to Emma to look after, I ran across the track for a better view. I scanned the course as Stony completed the first circuit safely, but tediously, and typically, he made no impression on the leaders. The second circuit was different. Tory got busy. Switching Stony to the inside the pair soon picked off several in front of them. Pulling away towards the third last she was now several lengths ahead. Tracking her with venom, however, was course specialist Ruby Flame under Michael Tory's daughter, Mouse.

Tory took a quick look behind and gave Stony a nudge; he quickened, increasing his stride.

They're going to win, shot through my mind.

And then *disaster*! Gasps from the crowd as Stony blundered onto his nose at the penultimate, catapulting Tory onto his neck. But fortunately, no! Not quite disaster. Losing the lead now to Ruby Flame, Tory quickly recovered, and the legs began to work. They jumped the last neck and neck.

Go on, Stony, I urged silently, clenching my fists, and so he did. He remembered his lessons with Dick, dug in, stretched out his neck, and won comfortably by eight lengths.

There was delight all round as the pair returned to the paddock and the winner's enclosure, apart, that is, from Ruby Flame's connections, which included racehorse breeder and owner Mrs Rachel Jowett. Rachel was to become Tory's future mother-in-law, but of course neither of them knew that then!

After a season with Dick, Tory teamed up with friends near Brackley and Stony moved to Graham Pidgeon and his daughter Jenny's yard in Northamptonshire. Jenny had been champion point-to-point jockey, and Graham was a founder member of the Point-to-Point Owner's Association, and had produced hundreds of winners, mostly ridden by Jenny. There was always one prize guaranteed with Denstone Wanderer. Big and beautiful, he glided around the parade paddock with perfectly plaited mane and tail, smart blue rug, edged in black with my initials stitched on – SML – it matched his smoky colour perfectly. Stony held his head high and looked around regally. He was supremely eye-catching, and whatever was to happen in the race, there was always a certain prize for Stony – the Best Turned Out.

Well that's it, he thought. *Job done. Back to munch hay and relax in my comfortable stable.*

Then out came the jocks. The bell rang. Tory was legged up smartly, a sharp reminder down his shoulder.

'Wake up, Stony – you've a race to run.'

And with that off they cantered to the start, his jockey crouching like a limpet in the plate, meaning business.

Stony was not a straightforward ride for Tory. He was big, she is little. He required pushing and shoving throughout the race. In 1994 the feature race at Tweseldown was the City of London race for amateur riders working in the City. Again Tory was the only lady rider and they were not expected to win, but urging Stony on like a demon all the way, he overtook several good horses, edged his way to second, and was set to challenge the leader, a multiple course winner and favourite, Alpha One, the former ride of Johnny Greenall. Excitement welled up and I prepared to celebrate. Winning was now the expected. But as the saying goes, 'horses are great levellers,' and so it proved. Stony ploughed through the last fence, bits of brush flying, and Tory popped off very neatly onto the track as the field streamed past, and I watched Stony gallop away on his own towards his horse box – and his hay net. Frustrating, but there is always another day.

At the end of that season Stony was turned out in the fields at the Pidgeons' farm. He had earned his holiday, and we looked forward to plans for next year, which included a Hunter Chase. But then a bitter blow struck. Stony, perhaps not the quickest of thinkers, was kicked in the field by another horse, and suffered a broken leg, with the inevitable consequences. He was a gentle horse and did not deserve this, but it demonstrated once again with piercing reality, how horses can touch our strongest and deepest emotions at completely opposite ends of the spectrum.

Denstone Wanderer

TWELVE

THAMESDOWN TOOTSIE

The rainbow bubble had burst. We had lost two horses within months of one another. With the loss of Folly, Polly's eventing career had taken a dip. Added to this Christopher and I were no longer able to finance her to the same extent as we had before. Neil Hansford had moved on from TNT, and this valuable sponsorship came to an end. However, she turned the setback into a new challenge, and with the initial assistance of Nick Pembry, and later Sue Hunter, she successfully set up her business at Charlton Park, producing International event horses, and finding new sponsorship with gun makers Holland and Holland.

Both Stony and Folly had been in their prime, and their loss left a gaping hole. But it is no use trailing round under a mantle of despair. Keep seeking the light at the end of the tunnel, and plug on. Sure enough, hope was reignited and what remained of a stuttering glow grabbed the wick, and leapt into a bright flame in the shape of a small bay person called Thamesdown Tootsie. She was, of course, a horse – a gritty little racehorse with a defiant mind of her own.

After Stony's death, Graham Pidgeon set about finding another horse for Tory. Methodically he scoured the sales catalogues, and with his experienced eye spotted a horse coming up at the Malvern Bloodstock sales that matched what he was looking for. It was October 1994, and on the day of the sale I waited keenly for a phone call. Had the bidding gone their way or not? At last the phone rang. It was Tory.

'We won the bidding for the horse, but she has failed the vet.'

Sickening, I thought.

'However, Graham is negotiating with the owner. She larked about at the sales and knocked herself. We are getting a second vet's opinion.'

All was not lost, and good news soon came. Thamesdown Tootsie was given the thumbs up, and she was purchased privately from Lambourn trainer, Anthony Jones, and away we went.

Thamesdown Tootsie stood no more than 15.2hh. Formally with champion jockey, Stan Mellor, she had won and been placed under rules. She was well-bred by the American sire Comedy Star out of Lizzie Lightfoot by Hotfoot. Neat and sharp, we were soon to discover she was also bold and resolute. Her size alone made riding her an easier challenge for Tory than Stony, and their temperaments matched. We were not to know at that point what a whirlwind of thrills she had packed in her small frame in that first point-to-point season.

Tory hunted and qualified Tootsie with the Grafton at weekends, and with the Bicester mid-week. Keen and competitive, the little horse was not difficult to get fit. Jenny boxed up to Nigel Twiston-Davies's yard to use his all-weather gallops, and I met them there a few times to watch the horses zip up the prepared track in pairs. I enjoyed these outings. Coupled with watching beautiful creatures displaying all their speed and power, the imagination is at work wondering how these horses might operate on the racecourse.

Thamesdown Tootsie had her own ideas. Unlike Denstone Wanderer, who excelled at showing himself off in the parade paddock,

Tootsie did not see the point, and agitated to get onto the course. Leaving the paddock to canter down to the start, along with the rest of the field, was a non-starter. Snatching at the bit, yawing and yanking, Tootsie danced sideways, leapt skywards and was generally quite impossible. Consequently permission was given for her to be led off early, and wait for the others at the start.

Tootsie was backed down from 33/1 to 10/1 at her first meeting at Kingston Blount, the site of the Oxford University Club point-to-point, and that is where we headed on February 4th 1995. Situated at the foot of the Chiltern Hills, the course is undulating with a steep stamina-testing incline, which had to be tackled twice on the way round.

The popular television series, *Downton Abbey*, featured Kingston Blount race course with a 1920s scene of a point-to-point. Local hunting followers took part as extras, along with the stars, which included the ice block Lady Mary on a rotund horse that looked as if it was about to drop a foal, rather than gallop three miles across the countryside. The scene was reminiscent of Siegfried Sassoon's *Memoirs of a Fox-Hunting Man*. Point-to-pointing as it was around the time of the First World War. Top hats or bowlers were de rigueur along with tweed and cavalry twill. Ladies riding astride was still considered rather 'fast'! Consequently, avoiding the disapproval of the indefatigable Dowager Duchess, played of course by the equally indefatigable Dame Maggie Smith, Lady Mary turned up immaculately attired riding side-saddle. The end of the race showed her ladyship having supposedly galloped through mud and over hedge, without a hair out of place or a ruffle anywhere. A sweaty brow with a flush on her cheek, or a spatter of mud would have looked quite realistic.

And so we return to the real thing at Kingston Blount. I should by now have got used to the noise, as a rushing cavalcade wing the birch at full force. Racehorses are not show jumpers, they need to jump reasonably close to the top of the fence to save time in the air. The whoosh and frequent thwack as they do so is dramatic. If you have a horse running, and find yourself standing next to a jump as many hooves thunder closer, it is heart in your mouth stuff.

Tootsie was entered for the Ladies' Open race with a large field of seventeen runners. Always impatient, she leapt smartly away as the flag went down. Close behind came Alice Plunkett on Military Two Step, followed by course winner and favourite, Green Archer. It was a bright, sunny day but there had been plenty of rain, and the going was heavy and holding. This suited a nimble Tootsie, and she skipped over the top of the turf. By the second circuit she was twenty lengths ahead of the field, and enjoying herself. But there remained five more fences, and Green Archer was galloping with relentless determination and getting ever closer. Had Tory gone too early? Twenty lengths narrowed to ten, and then to five. The favourite was quickening all the time. Shouts and whoops resounded all around, as the heavily backed Green Archer challenged coming to the last; but Tootsie was having none of it; she stuck her head out, held on and won by just three lengths. Stony had sadly gone, but this little rocket was promising something special.

Winning is addictive. Until then, you are happy to enjoy the partaking, and there is always hope, dreams perhaps, or the wish for a better run next time. After a win, anything else is just a sigh of relief that they have come back safe, and sound. It is not till the next day when the horse is brought out of its stable to be checked, and you scrutinise, as it is trotted up towards you, hopefully without a nod of the head, indicating pain somewhere in a foreleg, and then it is trotted away from you, without a dip in the hindquarter indicating pain behind. The latter is not often too worrying, but the former, where half a ton of horse lands over a jump on those delicate forelegs, always brings a concerned furrowing of the brow, and usually a call to the vet.

Pent up with the knowledge that Tootsie had proved she could win – and in style – we headed north to Weston Park on February 17th for the West Shropshire Drag Hunt point-to-point. Seat of the Earls of Bradford, Weston Park is situated in 1000 acres of rural Staffordshire, and the course runs through Capability Brown parkland with an abundance of mature trees and lakes, making viewing attractive but a little scratchy.

1995 continued wet, and the Staffordshire clay was well churned up. Once more we waited in the paddock for the horses to gather for the ladies' race. Tootsie, on her toes and bouncing, was led in with the other runners. She looked small compared with the horses alongside her, but she was beautifully proportioned, like a prancing show pony, or one of those perfectly modelled Julip horses that children love to play with. They left the paddock and a large field cantered past me down to the start. I waited and peered nervously through the trees, and fiddled with my programme. Then, realising the flag must have dropped, I sharpened up as a tightly bunched stream of horses came into view, going very fast indeed. I spotted Tory's light blue colours along with Tootsie's sheepskin breastplate, and watched catching my breath as several horses rose together over the brush. Tootsie landed safely, galloped on with the rest, and I breathed again.

The Ladies' Race is often the fastest of the day, the theory being that the girls cannot hold half a ton of surging horseflesh, galloping flat out at around thirty miles an hour. Tootsie, with not a very long stride, was stretched, but keeping in touch. At this stage the outcome looked an open book. As they entered the second circuit the pattern changed. The track had turned earth brown rather than grass green, and glistened with wet, cloying mud. Stamina and fitness was at the limit, the field were starting to flounder, and there followed a couple of crashing falls, but Tootsie was still there. Tory saw her chance, and crouched lower in the saddle.

'Come on, Tootsie.' And she squeezed her harder.

The horse accelerated like a tightly wound up clockwork mouse, leaving the field withering behind her. Within seconds she was way ahead and running her own race. Now with a good view, my eyes glued to the little bay figure sprinting between the fences, I heard the commentator.

'The field are entering the second circuit and Thamesdown Tootsie is moving up fast, and has taken the lead from Fell Mist, who has made much of the running. Katherine Swindells and Simply Perfect are not far behind. This is where Thamesdown Tootsie likes to be – at the head of affairs. Now with an impressive lead she is clear – *well* clear. She is forging on, increasing the gap. Approaching the last, she is a long, *long* way ahead of her rivals.'

Tory had nearly been caught at Kingston Blount, but this time she had waited before making her challenge. Tootsie was never the fastest, but with her accurate jumping, bottomless stamina and fierce determination to get her head in front, and stay there, she had outrun the whole field, winning with ease by fifteen lengths. I ran to meet them, and Tory punched the air as they galloped through the finish. Tootsie, still full of running, marched her way into the winner's enclosure, and a delighted Jenny ran across with red hair flying.

It's the taking part that counts, not the winning. Well yes, and no. Taking part is exhilarating and fun, that is why we do it. However priest John Daly, a keen racing man like many from the Emerald Isle, said with a twinkle, 'Ah well. Taking part is important, but it would be very *boring* if no one tried to win – that is the excitement – so it is!'

The Flint and Denbigh point-to-point was to be held three weeks after Weston Park, on Sunday 11th March at Eaton Hall on the Grosvenor estate near Chester. Plans soon got underway for Tootsie's third race. This was an important meeting for us. The Flint and Denbigh Hunt had been our early training ground, and we were looking forward to bringing Tootsie up from Northamptonshire to race. There was, however, to be some difference of opinion. It had rained relentlessly that year, and two days before the meeting it was still raining. Tory and Jenny made all the decisions regarding Tootsie's racing, but on this occasion I waded in. After entering, usually a week before the meeting, declarations to race or not can be made on the day. On the Friday before the meeting I had three phone calls. The first was from Tory.

'Jenny is not keen to bring Tootsie up for the Flint and Denbigh.

The forecast is terrible, the going will be terrible, and she does not want to risk her getting beaten.'

'How do you feel about it?' I asked.

'I want to race her,' Tory said.

'I agree, if she gets beaten so be it. I am so looking forward to seeing you both race at the F and D. It's a personal thing.'

'Well, be prepared. Jenny will be ringing you any minute.'

Sure enough the next call was from Jenny. Now Jenny Pidgeon is a forthright person. She also has rather fiery red hair.

'I do not wish to risk Tootsie on Sunday.' The tone was short and to the point.

There ensued a battle of words, but I was the registered owner, and in the end she had to back down. My insistence on running Tootsie on this particular occasion would be a classic example of 'It is the taking part not the winning that matters'. Tory and I were keen to race at the Flint and Denbigh. We would know lots of people, and it was our old stamping ground. I was proud of horse and jockey and I wanted to show them off. What happened on the day would be in the lap of the gods, or more likely in the feisty frame of Thamesdown Tootsie.

Finally, I had a third, rather unexpected call. The voice at the other end announced they were a member of the Swindells family. Now the Swindells in Cheshire have a history of winning point-to-pointers. I did not know them, but I had heard the name.

'Will you be running Thamesdown Tootsie on Sunday?'

'Yes,' I said. 'We are planning to.'

'Oh right. Thanks for giving me your decision.'

The response had sounded surprised and rather disappointed. Perhaps they did not want to risk losing the race, and assumed we would not be coming up to Cheshire with Tootsie in those conditions. Tootsie's two previous eye-popping wins meant she was fast becoming a very hot favourite indeed. We had decided to take our chance and race, and as forecast the windscreen wipers were working overtime, whipping back and forth across the dripping glass, as the Pidgeons' horse box pulled into Eaton Hall.

Despite the wet there was a good crowd parked several rows deep all the way alongside the final half mile of the track – fortunately on hard core, as it had been an air strip in the past. The usual 4 x 4 gatherings were taking place with families, friends, alcoholic picnics, children and dogs. There were Barbours, binoculars, betting tickets, and shooting sticks. Everyone was making the best of the weather, and keenly thumbing through the soggy programmes to see who was running. There was a sea of umbrellas and rainwear of every description. Water dripped from marquees. Tents flapped in the blustery wind, and bookies tried to keep the chalk dry by their boards. Horses and jockeys returned to the paddock from the racecourse with faces splattered with mud like spotted dog puddings. Meanwhile Tootsie, dry and cosy in the box, could hear the familiar sounds of a race meeting outside. Ears cocked, head up listening, she knew why she was there, and she waited impatiently for her turn.

The Ladies' Race was towards the end of the card, and with a break in the clouds a thin streak of blue sky was just visible, but the parade paddock was a quagmire, a morass of sloppy mud, slapping and sucking as the horses were led round, some skittish with anticipation, and tightly held by the lads and lasses slipping and sliding, trying to keep their feet. Hoardings advertised local companies, and I recognised race sponsor's names. Miles Macadum from Malpas and estate agents Jones Peckover. Banners announced the International Sheep Dog Trials, which would be held that year in Wales. I spotted familiar faces from our days in Denbighshire. Pressure was mounting. I so hoped Tootsie would run well, but the going was causing trouble in the earlier races.

Taken down to the start before the others, I noticed Jenny had tied up Tootsie's tail, knowing that wet mud would be thrown up in dollops from flying hooves around her, and also by her own. Having an earth-caked, wringing wet tail flapping around her hind legs could irritate her. Jenny was punctilious. Everything had been thought of. The little horse must be given every chance.

I made my way towards the track, and watched as the horses lined up. I saw Tootsie in the middle, her head high, ready for action. I recognised horses that had raced against her at Weston Park and Kingston Blount; Fell Mist and Heidi Brookshaw's Inch Maid among them. Was it possible Tootsie could be beaten this time? But there was no time for negative thinking. The starter climbed onto his rostrum, the flag was raised, a pause, then down it came, and the field surged forward as one. But quick as a heartbeat Tory switched to the inside, and took up the lead. There was plenty of pace and the wet going had an immediate impact. The field split, the first five pulling away impressively. Screwing up my eyes I saw the stream of colour stretching on into the distance, but Fell Mist and Tootsie were edging ahead. Stride for stride, nostril to nostril, not a breath between them, they were now twenty lengths ahead of the pack.

Galloping past the judge on the second circuit, it had become a two horse race. The next bunch, led by Love on the Rocks, looked hopelessly pedestrian. Behind these there was carnage. I am gripped with excitement. Tootsie is in her element. Whipping through the sloppy mud, she refuses to notice it. With Tory hugging tight to the rails at every opportunity, they increase their lead to thirty or even forty lengths from the field. There is only Fell Mist in between, and he is now fifteen lengths behind Tootsie. But there is still a mile to go, and Fell Mist is tracking her with ferocity. He throws down a challenge, and shortens the lead to five lengths. Can Tootsie possibly keep up this incredible pace? Will Fell Mist catch her? Not a chance. Tootsie is laughing. With four fences to jump, she pulls away yet again. I can see her but I can barely watch. I hear the commentator, his voice rising with excitement.

'The light blue jacket of Thamesdown Tootsie is now on her own out there, jumping from fence to fence and *still* going strong.'

Continuing, his voice quickens and the decibels rise again.

'Tory Lyon is coming to four out and a *BIG* bold jump from the leader. There are three left to jump, and *ANOTHER* bold jump from Thamesdown Tootsie. Now into the bottom turn, and swinging into the home straight, they come to the penultimate and – pause, pop over it neatly. This is now a one horse race. *Surely*, the pair must just jump the last.'

Through fingers stretched tight across my face, I watch and wait for the final fence, and listen.

'Tight held, coming to the last, and Thamesdown Tootsie jumps it perfectly. She has demolished the opposition. This is a *very* impressive win indeed.'

The spectacle of horse and jockey scorching their way round that energy-sapping track was extraordinary and utterly thrilling. Tootsie had confounded all doubts. She and Tory had galloped their rivals into the ground. Drenched with sweat, blowing hard, steaming and earth-caked, the horses made their way back to the paddock and, once again, Tootsie took her expected place in the winner's enclosure. Tossing her head, and stamping an impatient hoof, she kicked up at the mud stuck to her belly. The saddle was removed from her dripping back, and Tory went to weigh in.

'Weighed in, weighed in, horses away, horses away,' the tannoy called out.

All was in order, and Tory proudly carried off the cup for the Flint and Denbigh Ladies' Race, amongst rain-soaked smiles and applause.

Tootsie was unbeaten that year, and went on to win again at the Oakley Hunt point-to-point. Following that she battled gamely in a grinding finish to score at the Cheshire Forest Hunt at Tabley in Cheshire. She had achieved an undefeated nap-hand. Five wins in a row. She had proved herself a star performer. There were glowing reports in the racing press; Tootsie was rated champion mare in the South Midlands, and in the *Sporting Life Review*, she was among the author's top twenty point-to-pointers for that season. Two others were Eastern Destiny, who won two Cheltenham Foxhunters, and Cool Dawn, who later won the Cheltenham Gold Cup.

On her retirement Tory took Tootsie hunting with the Wilton, the Blackmore and Sparkford Vale and the Beaufort. She then went on to produce five foals. The first, a filly, was by a successful eventing stallion standing in Somerset. This chestnut mare turned out to be an out and out madam, and spent most of her time on her hind legs. However, three others, Mister Slipper, Mister Teddy and Mister Tiger, were notable successes on the racecourse. They were all by different sires. These were Midnight Legend, Tamure, and Emperor Fountain. Tootsie would spend her final days with me, and I would be lucky enough to own the last of her offspring – Mister Tiger.

Thamesdown Tootsie

THIRTEEN

HIGHLAND ROAD RETURNS –
FOLLOWING THE BEAUFORT –
TOPPING

As agreed with Count Borromeo, Highland Road flew back to us on his retirement from competing in Italy. He held celebrity status among his stable companions at Polly's base, Charlton Park, where he would enjoy hunting with Lady Suffolk and the great and the good of the British hunting fraternity –the Beaufort Hounds. Charlton Park House dates back to 1607, and the estate is the home of the Earl and Countess of Suffolk and Berkshire. It is ideally situated in the VWH – Vale of the White Horse – hunting country, and adjacent to the Beaufort. It was a wonderful set-up for Polly, where she had access to the estate parkland and fields. The stable block is in an enclosed courtyard of mellow Cotswold stone, around a central lawn. Entering through a tall archway with clock tower opposite, the yard is partly cobbled with several stables housed indoors, with lofty ceilings and original blue brick stable floors.

After two seasons hunting Bumble strained a tendon, and another suitable hunter was required for Lady Suffolk; I began to make a search. Hunters of this quality are not easy to find. It must have impeccable manners, be a proven jumper and able to keep up with the best. Phone calls were made, and before long a friend of mine rang me. Duncan Smith runs a training yard with accomplished veteran John Marsden. They were based at that time at Henbury in Cheshire, and I had known them for several years.

'I think I know just what you are looking for,' said Duncan down the phone.

'It is a horse called Genesis, he was hunted with the Cheshires by Naome Ferranti. She has now retired from hunting and taken up carriage driving.'

I trusted Duncan's judgement, and we arranged a viewing.

I met Duncan at Henbury Hall and followed him with interest to the stables. There inside a corner stable was a very good-looking, quality grey horse. He looked just the ticket, and proved to be so. Genesis subsequently arrived at Charlton Park, and he and Linda hunted successfully many times with the Beaufort. She became very attached to him, and with his elegant head looking across the stable yard to the house, he was the apple of her eye.

It was not long after that I had a phone call and was asked to find a hunter for a wealthy couple who also hunted with the same pack. The woman wanted something for her husband who had recently taken up hunting. Could I find her something reliable was the request, but not too sharp, as he was rather new to the game. I arranged to go and see Joe Howard at Toppings Farm near the Vale of Lune in Lancashire. The woman's husband drove up north with a groom, and we met at Joe's.

Joe comes from generations of horse dealers. He had built up a tidy yard of quality animals, mostly from Ireland. Very tall, with wavy jet hair, he had a rolling sort of a gait, and a touch of the Romany about him with a dry sense of humour. Joe pulled out a couple of likely hunters for a novice, and my friend particularly liked one of them. The horse was chestnut with two white socks; an Irish three quarter bred with a steady temperament. The man was no rider, but the horse did not take advantage, and they jumped three or four reasonable fences. He took a few photos and went away, seemingly happy. The next day his wife rang me.

'My husband really liked the chestnut horse,' she drawled down the phone.

'But you see *my* horse is grey, and it would be so lovely for us to be a pair, *doo* you think your dealer chappie might have it in grey?'

How ridiculous, I thought. *We were looking for a horse, not shopping in Bond Street.*

It was around this time that Camilla Parker-Bowles, as she was then, was being followed everywhere by the press. She hunted with the Beaufort on a charming little horse called Mollie. In order to avoid a barrage of pressmen, she decided to stable Mollie at Charlton Park with Polly. Hunters from Charlton had to be turned out immaculately. One day Polly was short-staffed. She asked me if I would plait up Mollie, and drive the horse box with Camilla to the meet. In fact the plan was not to go to the meet at all, as it would have been heaving with pressmen, but to go to a pre-arranged quiet spot about a mile away, and wait for the field to appear.

It was a long time since I had plaited a horse, as there were usually well trained students for this task. I arrived at the yard in good time and began to plait Mollie. As I finished my last plait, Polly walked into the stable. Staring at Mollie, she exclaimed, 'For heaven's sake, Mother, you've plaited her on the wrong side!'

Indeed I had. Horses are correctly plaited on the right side of their necks, not the left as I had done. Every plait is sewn in, and each one had to be undone and re-plaited on the correct side. Time was running on, and a student was quickly sent to assist, and while I began at the wither she stood on a bucket and started at the poll (top of the head). We completed as Camilla arrived, quite flustered as she had had to dodge a shadowing car. Mollie and her plaits looked splendid, and we boxed her up. Mrs Parker-Bowles then climbed up into the cab, and off we went.

Hounds were meeting in Tetbury. It was a bright and crisp morning, and I decided to follow by car with my terrier, Sparkle. I parked with other followers down country lanes, and gazed over typical Beaufort country of open fields and Cotswold stone walls. We saw no fox but soon hounds came streaming across, and then a huge field of galloping horses fanned out to tackle the stone wall, a vivid array of colour with the familiar blue and buff of the Beaufort Hunt. It was a splendid sight, reminiscent of a Lionel Edwards painting. Eventually, with a lull, the field drifted towards the gate onto the lane.

I had noticed earlier a couple of shiny, dark green Range Rovers. Range Rovers are not unusual amongst hunt car followers, often rather muddy, plus Land Rovers, Subarus, small cars, and bicycles. I even saw an ice cream van once, joining the car followers with the Devon and Somerset Stag-hounds on Exmoor. But these Range Rovers were spanking clean and polished. There were also several antennae in the form of extra tall aerials waving about from the rear and the roof, and the smart man sitting in the passenger seat had a phone planted to his ear. Mobile phones were not that common in those days. I don't think they were carrying a picnic basket in the boot either.

Soon it became apparent why these two vehicles were keeping so close to the action. Several mounted followers came trotting down the lane towards us, and with them came HRH Prince Charles. As the field went past, he glanced across and recognised two farmers standing with their bicycles in the narrow lane; pulling up his horse he hacked the few paces back, and took time to chat to them for a while, as the rest of the mounted field carried on. The two estate or farm workers must have so appreciated this thoughtful gesture.

I had agreed to entertain my young grandson, Freddie, for the day. Pushing a swing at the local playground did not appeal to me, so I said, 'Freddie, we are going for a picnic, but we are going to pretend we are lost in the wilderness, and we have to go hunting for our food. We will take Sparkle and Pickle to help us hunt for rabbits.'

Freds thought this a great idea, and with a good supply of chocolate treats plus Coca Cola, along with the picnic, we piled into the car with the dogs. Hounds were meeting nearby, and my plan was to follow in the car. Freds had great fun collecting twigs to make an imaginary fire, and shooting pretend pheasants and rabbits. However, at the first hint of action I bundled him back into the car, the chocolate bribes coming in very useful at this point. I really hoped we might see a fox, and we waited quietly for ages in a tree-lined lane, along with several other followers. Freds was getting a bit restless by now – so more chocolates were passed to the little boy in the back. Suddenly out from the trees and onto the lane slid Charlie, as quiet and slinky as could be.

'Freds, quick, look,' I whispered loudly.

He turned his head as the fox disappeared into the trees the other side, while Pickle was throwing herself at the shut window in ecstasy. We had had some fun and it was time to go home, so feeling pleased and uplifted, I taught Freddie a ditty or two, and together we chorused, 'Do ye ken John Peel' and 'A hunting we will go' all the way home.

When I told Polly about Freddie's new repertoire she said, 'Well I don't think that will go down very well at nursery!'

These instances were of course before the hunting ban dragooned into a law of lunacy by Tony Blair.

If your star horse trots up one day with a nod of the head – i.e. lame – panic calls to the vet will ensue, and probably to the farrier too; but you also need the 'back man'. Horses frequently suffer problems in the back – known as the 'top line', from the poll between the ears, to the rump and the base of the tail. These sometimes arise from initial injuries lower down in the feet or to the legs. Our back man in those days was Ronnie Longford. We visited his rustic cottage down winding lanes, where he produced a little wooden hammer, and a box to stand on, and proceeded to tap, tap, tap along the horse's spine, and then give it a shove, and some more taps, and then another shove. I soon learnt that Ronnie was a magician with horses. As a boy he went to school every day on his pony, and had learnt his craft from his father, who had cared for hundreds of horses on the battlefront during WW1, with minimal and basic veterinary equipment. Ronnie – whose official title is a chiropractor – was also an expert on herbal remedies, one of which was to wrap a cabbage leaf round an inflamed joint. Comfrey was another favourite. He was renowned in the racing and the eventing world, and in 2006 was awarded an MBE for his services to horses.

For some people, there is of course the 'black box'. When it was explained to me that there were mystery people that you will never meet, or see, and if you send them a hair from your horse's tail, they will show it to the black box, and this will miraculously reveal the problem, I laughed out loud. But for some, radionics is a legitimate form of healing. But to others, the very mention of a black box spells witchcraft. Is this a lot of jiggery-pokery, mumbo jumbo, faith healing, or is it an acceptable method of diagnosis? That is entirely up to the individual to decide.

I notice with interest a published list in the Badminton programme of horses that have completed Badminton four or more times over a span of sixty-five years, 1949-2014, and how comparatively few there are. Included in this list of equine alumni is a horse called Topping.

It was many years ago when I first travelled to Joe Howard's yard near the Lune Valley to view a four year old Irish horse.

'I am looking for something by Ballinvella,' I said to Duncan Smith one day. We were at Thirlestone Horse Trials in Scotland.

'I know of one,' Duncan said. 'It's up at Joe Howard's.'

Ballinvella was a stallion standing in Ireland with a reputation for producing 'jumpers' – horses with jumping ability. There is, of course, the theory that if you see a horse you like in Ireland, and ask what is the horse sired by, the answer may well be, 'Ahh well now, and what do you tink you would you loike it by?'

Soon I was off to see Joe. 'You've got a horse by Ballinvella, Joe?'

'Yup, ees a bit poor like, only had him two days but a good sort. I've got others mind.'

'Well let's have a look at him first.'

And with that, Joe pulled out a chestnut horse, red as a fox, with a broad white blaze down the length of his face, made more prominent because he had rather a Roman nose. He was not very big, just on 16 hands high, and lacking in condition, making his head look large compared to the rest of his body. Horses coming over on the ferry, from the bogs and outreaches of Southern Ireland, can sometimes have feet which are neglected, and have grown long. This horse shuffled along as if wearing slippers, rather than horse shoes. Hard as I tried to see a potential event horse, I just thought, '*What a strange-looking creature.*'

He carried his head low, he looked weary and resigned to whatever fate had in store for him. I felt rather sorry for him, and went to give him a pat on his neck. In that instant he changed. Up came his head, and turning towards me he cocked his ears, and looked me straight in the eye. There was something distinctly endearing and true about his expression. I thought in that moment, '*If you can jump, I will have you.*'

Well, he could jump. Over hedge, ditch and rails he bounded with obvious boldness. 'That will do,' I shouted to Joe across the field. I did not need to see any more. If I was to have him, with those feet, the sooner he was properly shod the better.

'How much, Joe?' I said.

'£4,500.'

'£4,000, and not a penny more.'

'Ees yours,' said Joe.

My new purchase did not have papers or a name. I gave him the name Topping, relating to Joe's house – Toppings Farm. I had an instinct it would suit him. He was one of many horses that I bought from Joe, plus a puppy, Tinker, which found her way to Tory and family.

'Ey up,' Joe said, watching, as I picked up a wriggling Jack Russell puppy from the litter of four in the stable.

'I thorrt it were a bitch you wanted.'

Turning it over, I replaced the little boy puppy with a girl. The reaction after driving from Lancashire to Wiltshire, and presenting the Jowett family with a dog, rather than a bitch, could have been interesting – especially as a pretty name had already been chosen – 'Tinkerbell'. Later known as Tinker, and not to be confused with Tinker, our former horse.

Topping arrived at Charlton, and Polly successfully produced him from an uninspiring four year old to a four star Advanced horse, completing Badminton twice, and Burghley once with him. Keen supporters of eventing, William and Jean Russell, bought him from me, and he completed Badminton twice more with Oliver Townend. A clear cross-country within the time launched Oliver and Topping on to a place in the British squad for the European Championships, and the following year the pair finished sixth in the British Open at Gatcombe Park.

I have always liked the rags to riches element in Topping's story. His strength was the cross-country, and he was very fast. He was also brave, tough, and injury-free. He was a survivor. He was boss in the field, and enjoyed seeing off the Highland cattle at Charlton Park. Oliver pays tribute to him as the horse that earned him his first British flag.

FOURTEEN

THE COUNTRYSIDE MARCH – A NEW MILLENNIUM – BUMBLE SAYS GOODBYE – A FOAL ARRIVES

The fox looked out on a winter's night,
wishing that man would treat him right.
Allow him to roam and maybe to run,
But spare him the trap, the gas, and the gun

I met Clarissa Dickson-Wright a few times at the Cholmondeley Arms in Cheshire, a sporting pub which also claimed renowned Cheshire huntsman Johnnie O'Shea as a regular. I admired her delight in defying political correctness, her championing of the countryside and especially hunting. She had death threats several times from louts and loonies, and was once sent a card from the 'animal rights' activists threatening her life. Unfazed she picked up the telephone and said to them, 'I loved your card – can I order a hundred?' She led a band of supporters on the epic Countryside March in 2002 after first setting up a stall with hot bacon butties, or perhaps it was game butties. A huge supporter of the Countryside Alliance, Clarissa was fearless in defence of a way of life for the people of Britain's countryside.

I attended the first Countryside March in 1998, which was preceded by a massive rally of 120,000 people in Hyde Park on the 10th July, 1997. This was a show of strength from hunting supporters against the proposed hunting ban. I travelled from Wiltshire with Tory, Polly and huge numbers of VWH and Beaufort Hunt supporters on specially hired trains filled to the gunnels. Arriving at Hyde Park were hunt supporters as far as the eye could see, and floating brightly in the air were balloons, the names of packs of hounds etched on them so people could team up with their particular hunt. There was a great atmosphere of esprit de corps. At one end of the vast park a stage was set up with microphones, and on this, well known people were speaking, actors Edward Fox and Jeremy Irons among them, and the most riveting of all the Labour peer, Baroness Mallalieu, with a voice speaking deep from the heart. All in support not just of hunting, but of freedom, too. As she completed her speech, we heard music – I think it was pipes – coming closer and louder, and into view amongst great cheers from the crowd, came a proud contingent from Wales. They had marched for several days from the Principality. The whole experience was extraordinarily moving.

Five years later, with a Labour government in office, the ban on hunting looked likely, and the mood from the countryside had turned to defiance and fury. The second Countryside March, called Liberty and Livelihood, would take place in London on September 22nd 2002. The date was in the diary. Come hell or high water we would be there. I look at my keen hunting grandchildren now, and think little did they realise then, as tots, or not even born, the enormity of what was happening all those years ago. Of course, the ban is nonsense. Simon and Emma, along with thousands of others, are still hunting within the law, and I run through wet and muddy fields trying to keep up, dragged along by two terriers panting with eagerness. Pickle knows the sound of the horn, and I have to hang on to her tightly.

On the eve of the march Geoffrey and I travelled from Cheshire, and next morning caught the tube to the City for the start of the march. As we drew into the metropolis the sight that met us was extraordinary. London had been taken over and overwhelmed by the countryside of Britain. We joined a multitude of people making their way to the scheduled start point of the Livelihood section of the march. There were similar multitudes at the Liberty end. So massive were the numbers that it took us three shuffling hours to actually reach the start, but no one cared, there was great comradeship amongst us, and humour, too. We bumped into friends, and hailed people we knew across the crowds of heads. We shook hands with many we did not know, but everyone on the march was our friend that day.

With excitement mounting as we neared the official start, the thousands doubled as we met up with the Liberty crowd. Now we were engulfed with a roar resembling a battle cry from people fighting for their cause. Banners were held high, shouting out their messages. There were seas of them, some huge, held by six or more people, some small, held by children. There was a life-size puppet of a stupidly grinning Tony Blair with a banner round his neck. 'Man of straw', it said. There was the blast of hunting horns, whistles, hollering and cheers. People leant from the windows of tall buildings as we passed by, applauding and shouting encouragement. As we marched on, all around us were many rural groups. There were falconers, shooters, anglers, hunt servants, jockeys, farriers, vets, ferret owners, Pony Club members, as well as the hundreds of hunting representatives from Scotland to Cornwall. There were the smart ones – the Quorn and the Beaufort – and the Banwen Miners and the Fell packs from Cumbria.

There were dukes and earls, country tweeds and rustics, Liverpool rat catchers, gamekeepers and terrier men – one with a tri-coloured head sticking out of a bag across his back. There were babies in pushchairs, disabled in wheelchairs, children carried on shoulders, bright teenagers and elderly people with sticks. There was a man called Mohammed leading a group of Muslim hare coursers. There were representatives from twenty other countries who had gamely travelled by air and sea to support us; the Société de Vénerie from France, 400 members of the Live Oak Hounds flew in from Florida, and more from Australia, the continent and the Irish republic.

As we approached the Cenotaph, still noisy with cheers and horns, everyone fell silent in a show of respect, and men removed their hats. This gesture was impressive, and again demonstrated the decency of the country people who, on that day, were driven to anger and protest. My parents lived through the years of WW2. Growing up in the post-war years of the 1950s, the name Winston Churchill was one I heard frequently. For their generation he was a war-time political giant, a British lion, a saviour. There were commemorations in 2015 of the great man's magnificent state funeral, which took place fifty years before on January 30th 1965. I mention this because it struck me, as I watched the recording repeated on television, that if he had been alive and able, if not in person, he would most certainly have marched with us in spirit, and would have climbed onto that platform in Hyde Park, and delivered a monumental piece of oratory in support of everything we stood for – freedom and liberty, and for the millions of people representing the true countryside of Britain, which he loved and battled for. As he made his final journey by train from London, to be buried at Woodstock near his birthplace, Blenheim Palace, many people stood along the sixty-five miles of track as the train passed. A farmer standing on the bonnet of his tractor removed his hat. An old soldier, resplendent in uniform, plus medals, stood to attention on his balcony and saluted; and included amongst these en route, stood a branch of the Pony Club, all mounted and grouped together in respect.

Hunting has, of course, continued, and despite David Cameron's pledge in his election manifesto to provide a free vote to overturn an unworkable law, this did not happen. Although the majority of hunts manage to continue without incident, others find the situation very difficult. The stag hounds, and the foot packs in Cumbria, are continually pestered by unidentified people in balaclavas, and with studs in weird places.

With Tootsie in foal and out of hunting action, Highland Road waved goodbye to Charlton Park, and took up residence at Bake Farm in the village of Coombe Bisset, near Salisbury. Here he would be cared for like a prince by Tory, and go hunting with the Wilton hounds. Bumble and Polly had been friends and unique partners in their story of sparkling success, but now in his twilight years he would transfer this allegiance to Tory. With the strict diet and disciplined training of three-day eventing behind him, he could be indulged and allowed titbits. He relished all the attention and whinnied when he heard the door open and Tory making her way to the stables. She hunted him with the Wilton hounds for three seasons and also, and I quote, 'If I fancy a bit of fear I set off with Roger (Roger Jowett – Tory's father in law) to the Portman vale.'

Adjacent to the Wilton, this part of the Dorset country is noted for some very big hedges with ditches.

'Follow me,' hailed a portly thruster, on a plunging middleweight.

Weighing up the black hedge, Tory gave Bumble a nudge with the spur and prepared to do that very thing. However, the portly thruster never took off, and an impatient Bumble sailed over horse and rider in the ditch, plus towering hedge, in one leap – well, he had been round Badminton.

The popular Wilton hunt show was coming up, and Tory entered Bumble in the Veterans class. With his coat buffed up and mane neatly plaited, he spun around the arena, flicking out his toes in an extended trot just like a pro. Announced the winner, he stood once more in his accustomed place at the head of the line, and Tory was handed some weighty silver ware. Bumble then galloped past triumphantly, with a bright red rosette flying from his bridle. He celebrated his 21st birthday at a party at Polly and Toby's house in Tetbury. Meeting many of his human friends over the years, he munched the grass and enjoyed a piece of cake.

A moment in history arrives. Fireworks emblazon the sky all around the world. It is January 1st 2000 and we enter a new millennium. In the same year a phone call arrives for me here in Cheshire from Salisbury. It is Christo, my son-in-law. The date is the 1st November 2000. All Saints day, and there is a new arrival in our family. Is it a foal? Or perhaps it's a puppy. But no – two legs, not four, and it is called Simon. I am somewhat daunted. I quote the unforgettable words of Margaret Thatcher on the birth of her first grandchild. 'We have become a grandmother.' It was a few days after that phone call that I had another – rather different. It was Christo again. 'It's Bumble,' he said. 'He has had an attack of colic, the vet is with him now and so are my parents and Phillipa.'

Christo's parents Roger and Rachel are experienced horse owners and Phillipa is their conscientious groom. I knew Bumble had caring and knowledgeable people with him. Christo continued, 'Bumble is not looking good, and I do not want to worry Tory,' who was still in hospital, with Simon.

Colic in a horse can be a serious condition and I knew I had to think quickly. If bad enough a twisted gut can occur, requiring surgery. What is known as dropping a horse, which essentially means anaesthetising a large animal sufficiently, before hoisting it up for surgery, can be a risk. A specially designed padded operating theatre is required as half a ton of animal goes down unconscious, and I knew not all horses recovered from colic surgery. 'What is the opinion of the vet?' I said, pacing the room, phone grasped to my ear. 'Bumble is not good,' repeated Christo. 'The vet does not advise operating at his age.'

I hesitated, imagining them all in Bumble's stable waiting for my reply. I knew the decision I had to make, hard though it was. I drew reassurance that Bumble was in his familiar stable with friends. I gave Christo my reply and put the phone down. Perhaps it was easier for me as I was not in that stable in those last minutes, but I felt a sort of thankfulness. Bumble had had such a rewarding and star-spangled life, and over the next few days I comforted myself that perhaps he had made the decision himself – a new life had arrived in Tory's life. It was now his time to say goodbye. Yes, I pondered – he was always a horse of intelligence and generosity. He was twenty-two years old.

Let us move on a few years. It is autumn 2016. Brilliant colours emblazon the trees; fiery red and gold against a gunmetal sky, but the nights are drawing in. Shivering a little in the chill, I peer through the window into the descending shroud of dusk. There appears the dim outline of a small horse standing by the hedge, no white except a star. Could it be the ghost of Tootsie in her familiar paddock? But the horse raises her head when I rattle the feed bucket, and canters over, kicking her heels. It is no phantom. Tootsie, doughty as ever, is still with us, and she will be thirty-two in January. This is her retirement home and I am her carer. She has not been idle in her retirement and has presented me with a foal, the last of five. That was ten years ago. I called him Mister Tiger after Tiger Woods – winner of the British Open Golf

Championships at Hoylake in 2006, the same week that Mister Tiger was born. Apart from my links with Hoylake, I hoped he might be a winner like the controversial golfer. His sire, Emperor Fountain, was a class horse and the sire of Cheltenham winner Frenchman's Creek, and thrice National Hunt winner Shillingstone.

As the day of Tootsie's foaling drew near, I kept a watchful eye on her. It would be a late foal; we were already in the month of July, and I had been banking up the sides of the stable with straw, when one morning there was no Tootsie looking over the door as usual. Something must be happening. Sure enough, Tootsie's foaling had begun. This usually happens in the quiet of night but Tootsie was an old hand, and I knew this one would not be long in coming. I ran indoors to ring the vet and in those few minutes when I ran back to the stable, I could see the first signs of the foal in its shiny white membrane,like a bag. If all is well, foals are born in a diving position with one hoof slightly in front of the other, followed by the muzzle, and I watched as the foal slipped out as easily as toothpaste from a tube. With both his dam and sire standing 16 hands high or less, this foal would not be big, but he was perfect, and within an hour was on his feet. Tootsie did everything. I just needed to check all was proceeding normally, and soon the vet arrived to double-check. I had a dark bay colt with a white star like his dam. What would the future hold? I was also aware that I had a thoroughbred colt to look after, and would need to handle this new baby right away.

The next day I put a foal slip on his dainty head and held him with my arms round his chest and hindquarters. Then I ran my hands up and down his spindly legs – like glass they were – and carefully picked up his hard little hooves. Tootsie watched me unconcerned, and I put a head collar on her and led her into the paddock, the foal trotting along glued to her flank. It did not take him long to discover the sense of space and the springy grass beneath his feet. Soon he was cantering round like a fairy with wings on his heels, while Tootsie followed in an anxious trot, whickering throatily to him all the time. She was a perfect mother, conscientious but, as he grew bigger, quite prepared to nip him if he became bumptious.

Unlike the majority of racehorses, who are born on a stud and live their early lives in a herd with other foals and their dams, Tiger's first year was spent in the paddock next to our house, with just his mother for company. He became quite humanised and sociable. He was curious about the goings on around him. Whenever the old cylinder mower came out he cantered over and watched, blowing softly through his nostrils, as this strange, oily-smelling green animal made its way, clanking and grunting, across the grass. The attractive Victorian building of the little village primary school is opposite the paddock, which has a gate onto the lane. Tiger soon had it worked out when the children arrived in the morning, and departed in the afternoon. Every day he made his way onto the grassy bank in the corner of the field which overlooked the school, and watched for his small friends. Then off he trotted to the gate and waited with pricked ears while children queued with carrots. Titbits are not a good idea with young horses, it encourages them to nip. However, Tiger was having such a lovely time I decided to ignore it, knowing that once he went into training, he would soon get a bop on the nose if he misbehaved.

Our paddock is also next door to the village church. One day I looked across to see a funeral in progress, and as the procession arrived at the graveyard, there, not six feet away, was Tiger, leaning over the post and rail fence, watching with great interest as the burial took place. The mourners stood solemnly while the priest gave the blessing, but I expect one or two must have smiled a little at the horse peering at them over the fence. He probably thought he was going to get a few carrots!

When Tiger was four years old I sent him to Sam Allwood. Sam had started to train point-to-pointers at his parents Robert and Rachel's farm at Ash Magna near Whitchurch. I did not know the Allwoods but I knew that Sam had twice been amateur champion in the West country, had ridden successfully under rules and done his

apprenticeship with two of the best trainers in jump racing – Phillip Hobbs and Robert Alner. It was a while since our racing days so I had done my homework and asked around, when someone said to me, 'If you want to win you should send your horse to…' and she mentioned a renowned trainer in the area. And then she said, 'But you won't know what is going on, you won't have a say in where your horse races and you won't really have a say in anything.'

I knew this would not suit me. Winning is the icing but I wanted to enjoy myself too, and I had been too long in the competitive horse world not to want to be involved in my horse's career and wellbeing.

From day one Sam has rung and updated me with good news or bad. I visited Tiger whenever I wanted and enjoyed a coffee and chat with the family, and I regularly watched Tiger on the gallops with other owners. Sam always discussed his plans, and my policy was to listen to him. He knew Tiger inside and out; he was riding him, training him, and looking after him. Coupled with all this the yard is immaculate, the horses shine and it was not difficult for me to see that the horses in Sam's care were paramount. During the years that Tiger was there, Sam had the invaluable backup of Robert and Rachel; driving the box, answering the phone, entertaining the owners, seeing the vet, filling in forms and so on. I know all about this because, of course, I have done it too.

As part of his early training, once the harvest was over Sam took Tiger on the many cross-country rides across the Cheshire farmland. I could not wait to see him on these nursery school outings. His next lessons would be out cubbing, or autumn hunting as it must be called today. I love the colours, the smells and sounds of autumn because it is the start of the hunting season. There is always a damp, musty feel as the year draws to a close, but beneath the dying foliage, new life is already preparing to spring up again, and once winter sets in, the spine-chilling bark of a fox will echo in the night as she calls for a mate.

With the alarm set at 5.30am and hounds meeting around 6.30am, somewhere in the depths of the North Staffordshire hunting country, I rouse a couple of terriers and, balancing a mug of coffee, off we set in the chilly mist of an October dawn. One of the best things about hunting is you can find yourself in parts of the countryside to which most people would never venture. Some of these places can be quite wild, and some may be part of private estates. It is often here, if you are quiet, you will experience the best sightings of the wild creatures of the countryside.

Watching young horses at the start of their careers is so full of hope. Sam gave Tiger confidence and taught him well, and the horse learned to jump everything he was asked. He loved his hunting and I loved seeing him out, holding inside myself that excitement and anticipation of the day I would see him on a racecourse. However, I am realistic. I was fully aware of the fact that many horses never make it to the racecourse, and many more will never get near the winning post. No other animal can be as unpredictable or injury prone as the thoroughbred racehorse.

Tiger's first race was at Barbary Castle near Marlborough on December 3rd 2011. He was five years old, and I look back on the experience as just a taster. However, I still felt a sense of pride watching him in the parade paddock, and noticing my name in the programme. I was just thrilled to finally see him on the race track. It had been a long time since that memorable day I had watched him slip into the world. As I have mentioned, until you win, everything else is just a relief that the horse has come back safely, and in one piece. Well, we did not win that day, but he returned injury-free and we still had the whole of the season in front of us. I could not at that stage anticipate the thrills my lovely horse had in store for me, but neither could I possibly have known the terror that lay ready to pounce, just five days after that first race, the day I picked up the phone and listened to Tory with words that shook me like a tempest.

'Polly has a head injury and is on life support.'

Overnight, Ward 1, the Intensive Care Unit at Frenchay Hospital, Bristol, became the pivotal place in my life.

FIFTEEN

EXTRACT FROM MY JOURNAL AT FRENCHAY HOSPITAL, BRISTOL

Pulling off the M4 Bristol motorway with a sense of urgency, Geoffrey and I drove into the bewildering complex of a large hospital, and I quickly scanned the mass of signs for the Intensive Care Unit; my antennae were acute, and it did not take long. The security doors swung open, and following a nurse past silent beds my eyes flicked up and down searching for Polly. She was propped up on a high bed at the top of the ward, semi-screened off. Eyes closed, unconscious, she was barely recognisable. Attached from her feet to her head to her finger tips were tentacles of tubes and wires coming out of her mouth, her nose, her arms, her chest, and her head. There were thick ones, thin ones, transparent ones, coloured ones. Above and at the sides of the bed were strange apparatus, monitors, ventilators and imaging screens. Polly lay still, but attached to her, around her, and keeping her alive, all was pulsating and throbbing. Zigzag lines like sharp peaks on a mountain range – different colours – red, white, blue, green, yellow, flashed across the black monitoring screens demanding attention. Blood pressure, oxygen, heart rate, brain pressure and so on. An insistent *beep – beep – beep* disturbed the heavy hush.

Doctors and nurses circled the bed, and after we arrived, Polly began to shiver and shake uncontrollably, which was very unnerving, and I wondered what was going on. This was her body attempting to come out of unconsciousness. She was immediately sedated, and put into a medically-induced coma. At midday Tory arrived from Salisbury. Her face pinched with anxiety, she was directed towards Polly's bed. They had always been close as sisters. I went to meet her and explained about our meeting with the consultant. Toby, Tory, Geoffrey and I met up in the bright, airy restaurant on the hospital campus. We had to discuss practical issues. There were animals and small children; I needed a car, as Geoffrey would return the next day to keep things going in Cheshire. I also needed a base, for how long I knew not. It was a strained and worried group. I tried to focus on the positive words of the consultant.

'She has age on her side and she is supremely fit.'

Saturday. I occasionally take my eyes off Polly, and notice what is happening around me. There are two Intensive Care Units – ICUs – with around six beds just down one side, and one at the top where Polly is. With further stages of recovery the beds get nearer the door. Frenchay Hospital was first built in the 1940s, for injured American servicemen based in this country during WW2. These ground level wards are reached by endless corridors with low ceilings, like walking through the London Underground. The walls are bare brick, and painted in odd colours; yellow, orange and beige with signs everywhere. Neuro surgery, Neuro theatre, Neuro science, Neuro Xray, Neuro scan etc.

Polly is reliant on the life support machines which interact with each other. She is fed through her nose. Her feet and legs have attachments which expand and deflate, to avoid lower leg thrombosis.

A tube in her throat drains fluid from reaching her chest. She has her own one to one specialist nurse twenty-four hours around the clock. I sit with her as the hours pass, willing her to wake up, but not a sign. Her nurse, Elaine, talks to her constantly, and tells her every time she ministers to her, 'Polly, I am going to take your temperature. Polly, I am going to shine a torch into your eyes. Polly, I am just going to press down on your eye lids, push my hand away, Polly – sorry Polly. Polly, open your eyes, Polly, squeeze my hand.'

The doctors were looking for responses to these stimuli. We had to prepare for disappointment. Each time there was nothing. She would stiffen her arms when the nurses pressed on her eyelids, but the reactions were involuntary – not what they were looking for. They wanted Polly to actively lift her arm and push them away.

With the apparatus, drips and charts, there is little room near the bed, but I find a chair and squeeze myself as close as I can. She does not appear to hear me, but I talk to her as normal. 'Hello Polly, I've just arrived,' etc.

She coughed as fluid built up in her throat, the zigzag lines shooting across the screen, lights flashing. They leap up, then down, and up again. They hover around 5 – 8, but I stare, terrified, as they jump to 14, then 18 – 20 – 40. 'Oh, please God, no higher.' Then down they go again, *beep, beep, beep*, and the mountain peaks, jagged and threatening, return to wavy lines, and the numbers drop to 5 – 7 – 9, and back to 5.

Sunday. The doctors have reduced the sedation, but increased it again as the brain pressure monitor went up. This is a balancing act. They want Polly to wake up without disturbance to the brain. It is a waiting game, and the not knowing is so hard to deal with. I have to be very, very patient. You have to force yourself to think positively, and simply not allow the 'what ifs' to encroach into your thoughts.

As I walked up the ward towards Polly, I noticed a young girl in one of the beds whom I had not seen before; she was smiling and had a huge black eye. A doctor and her parents were round her bed. I thought, she cannot be in Intensive Care because of a black eye, and unlike most of the other patients, she was fully conscious. Eventually I had a chance to speak to her parents. Only four days after Polly's accident, I was still in shock, and wrapped up in my own worries. 'What has happened to your daughter?' I enquired. I then listened, horrified, as her mother described that she was on her bicycle in Bristol, when a lorry knocked her over, and did not stop. This pretty twenty-two year old had lost a leg. She had been operated on after arriving at A and E only yesterday. I was trying to have courage in my own situation, and then this story hit me hard; here was a family going through such trauma with their daughter, too. She did not stay long in this neurological ward, but I did learn that she had had to have a second operation to remove more of her leg. I do hope she will be alright.

It is 4.35pm. Polly's temperature is high. Elaine is giving her paracetamol intravenously. Her right arm and wrist are swollen and bruised, due to the emergency probes that were inserted by the paramedics at the site of the accident. Elaine moves quietly but positively round the bed. Polly has her mouth rinsed three or four times a day with a menthol solution. She has Vaseline round her eyes. Her face is covered with a moisturiser, as are her neck and arms. Her nurses talk to her all the time.

'Sorry, Polly,' they say, if she reacts to something she does not like. She has cotton wool pads under the tubes stretched across her face to prevent pressure, and these are changed regularly. She does not like this at all, and reacts by shivering, and the coloured lines jump angrily across the screen. Despite being unconscious she can clearly feel discomfort. I want to stroke her arm to comfort her, but I resist, I don't want to add to the disturbance. She calms down, the beeping peters out, and there is just a regular flash now, like a lighthouse winking a warning in the night.

Monday 10.40am. I am in the hospital corridor trying to listen to my mobile phone. There is much activity with patients on trolleys, medics in white coats, nurses and hospital admin staff, visitors, families – some with strained faces, some chatting. Outside, ambulances blare with urgency. The place buzzes with the rhythms and routines of a busy hospital on a Monday morning. Very different to when I left yesterday late Sunday evening, making my way through the endless dimly-lit corridors, empty and rather eerie. But there is no change with Polly. I tell her it is me, hold her hand, mention a few familiar names, and then find a chair, and prepare for another long wait. There is a new male nurse today, Dominic. Polly looks so peaceful; her breathing, which I can see move up and down through the bulky ventilator on my right, is deep and regular, but oh how we long for a sign that she is ready to wake up. We just have to wait, and wait, and wait.

Tuesday 4.20pm. Polly has just had a bout of coughing, and with the tubes in her mouth and nose, she seemed to struggle for breath. The numbers on the monitor shot up to 35 then *50*. My hands clench, and I want to call out, 'Is she *alright?*' It has now returned to 9, and hopefully going down. I talk to Elaine for a while, and ask her about her job. She said that not all nurses can adapt to the ICUs. They find it too intense, the responsibility too great. This I can imagine. I think they have to be deeply committed, and I regard them with admiration.

I look at my watch, 6.20pm. Toby will arrive at 7.00pm. It is dark outside and sleeting. An hour and forty minute's drive to my base, Tory's home near Salisbury. Nothing is likely to change tonight. I gather my coat and prepare to leave on this, the sixth day, sitting, watching and waiting. I talk to Polly, and tell her I am going and will see her tomorrow. Can she hear me in the deep recesses of her mind? Who knows, but you have to keep trying. She lies still, eyes closed, breathing evenly but in another world. Tomorrow I return to sit, watch, and wait again.

Wednesday. It is nearly a week since the accident. Polly is now off all sedation but she is still in a coma. The consultants want some response, particularly movements which are not involuntary, as they have been so far. Worryingly, she has not shown positive reactions to any stimulus given. It is, as we have been told, a long haul and a long wait. We are still in the dark. I stare at her, looking for any tiny flicker. I talk to her as if she can hear me. I say familiar names. Freddie, Jack, Tag. I feel a lump in my throat as I write this, and still there is no response.

A nurse has just said the hospital Press Office requires my permission for a statement. I give a simple statement. 'Polly remains critical but stable.' There has been much about Polly's accident in the equestrian press, and on the internet, and also in the *Daily Mail* and *Express*. *Horse and Hound* reported there had been an overwhelming response of get well wishes on their website. A letter arrived from Buckingham Palace for Toby from the Queen; this was as a result of his three-year appointment as equerry to Her Majesty. She expressed her and Prince Philip's concern, and praised the medical team at Frenchay. Toby gave a copy to the nurses to pin up in their off duty sitting room.

7.00pm. I must leave soon. I watch Polly, hoping for a little sign of waking up before I go, but nothing. I linger, and look back at the bed. I must put my trust in the nurses and doctors, and wait through another night. It was dark as I entered the lit up but silent winter car park, it was empty and I felt very alone, but quickly gave Sparkle and Pickle a walk on the only patch of trodden grass. It starts to sleet again, and I gear myself up for the difficult journey to Salisbury. The roads are busy, wet, and slippery, with headlights blinding my vision all the way. Sparkle is an old dog now, and after an hour she paws at the window.

'We won't be long, Sparkies – can you wait?'

But I play safe, stretch for the lead, and pull into a field gateway, rain still sheeting. It is worth the journey, as Simon and Emma run up with a welcome, a steak awaits to be cooked by Christo, plus a glass of wine – or two.

It is nearly a fortnight since the accident, and I am entering the High Dependency Unit – HDU – where Polly has now been moved. I returned home for two days to recoup, and while away Tory rang to tell me that she had felt a flutter of a squeeze of her hand, and Polly's right eye had opened a crack. I hesitantly walked the length of the new ward, nervous of disappointment after Tory's update. I was directed to Polly, and as I approached I saw her right eye was just open a slit. I said, 'Polly, it's Mum,' as I reached the bed. She tried to smile, somewhat lopsidedly. I held her hand and she squeezed it just a little. Tory had been right, Polly had at last woken up. Everest had been conquered. I simply cannot describe the relief. I sat beside her, and she dropped off to sleep. I talked to her for a bit, but mostly just sat and wrote this. She sleeps most of the time. Every now and then I say, 'I am still here, Pols,' and she tries to smile.

It is the second day visiting Polly in the HDU. Again I am apprehensive. Will she be better, the same or worse? I steel myself, press the security button, the doors open, and I enter the brightly-lit ward. I look for Polly at the top; she is well propped up, and yes, she smiles crookedly when she sees me. All slight movement is coming from the right side; hand, eye, half smile. The physiotherapist, Louise, explains they will reduce the strength of the tracheotomy, encouraging Polly to breathe on her own. Once they remove this, she said, Polly will use her vocal chords and try to speak, but to start with it will not necessarily make sense – and she was right – it didn't. Quite funny now looking back, but at the time it was rather disconcerting.

As Polly sleeps, I look round the ward. The HDU is more bustling than the ICU; less of the tiptoed atmosphere and whispered voices. Nurses chatter to the patients, and as part of their work, they regularly ask them questions.

'What day is it? What year is it? What day is Christmas?'

Most are post-operative neurological patients in various stages of recovery. Opposite Polly, a man looks anxiously into the blank face of his relative, and I hear a nurse questioning, 'Denise, who is this come to see you? Denise, what month is your birthday? What is the Prime Minister's name? Come on, Denise, answer me.'

And so it goes on. Sadly, Denise does not seem to be responding, and the man stares into her closed eyes. Hygiene is paramount. Handwash pumps are placed at frequent intervals, with images of pink hands and words saying DON'T PUT PATIENTS AT RISK. DON'T INFECT – PROTECT. MAKE HAND HYGIENE YOUR PRIORITY.

24th December – Christmas Eve. Polly is inching forward slowly. She remains wired and tubed up, but less so. She is moving her head, and starting to notice what is happening around her. She is trying to mouth words, but there is no sound. Three nurses lift her into a special chair, and all the tubes and wires go with her. It is interesting how she locks on to the nurses who minister to her. We, her close family, are there visiting all the time, but she seems to instinctively know that it is the nurses who are so vital to her recovery, and her eyes follow them. There is a cheery air in the ward today, with nurses wearing tinsel in their hair. I tell Polly it is Christmas Eve; she nods, but seems confused.

Frenchay Hospital had now become a familiar place, and as I left one evening, I felt as if I had stepped from another planet. The hospital had become Polly's world, and for the past weeks it had been my world too. The never-ending corridors, the gloomy winter car park, the sterile wards, the silent beds behind security doors, and the blue uniformed nurses were everyday normal routine; a safe haven enclosed, shut away from the hectic world outside; the economy, foreign wars, the frantic rush, crazy glitter and bulging supermarkets of the Christmas bandwagon.

2nd January 2012. Polly has been transferred to the Brain Injury Rehabilitation Unit – BIRU – on the hospital campus. With no more tubes and wires attached to her, she now looks like Polly, and is in her own clothes. She will remain here for about four months. She recognises people, and is chatty but still very confused, and she has to learn to walk again. She has said she is bored, and one day asked the nurse for her coat. 'I must go and lunge a horse!' she insisted.

As predicted, Polly remained at BIRU for over three months.

Once here, the doors opened for all visitors, and these came aplenty and often. Friends were incredibly thoughtful, and as well as visits; cards, letters, flowers kept coming too. It took her a long time to walk unaided, but with the unstinting and expert rehabilitation that Polly received, she slowly got better. A large percentage of her recovery was due to her own discipline and determination. I recall her saying to me, 'Once it dawned on me I was stuck in a wheelchair, I decided, I've *got* to get out of this infernal thing.'

Nor did she like being cooped up indoors. Tory gamely pushed her around the large hospital campus I don't know how many times. This procedure proved difficult. Designed to be used round the wards on small wheels, outside, on uneven terrain, was akin to pushing a laden supermarket trolley across a twisty cross-country course – this wheelchair had a mind of its own – rather like its occupant.

There were innumerable gestures of kindness to Toby and Polly during her months of hospitalisation. With the gales preventing the air ambulance from taking off safely, former student Hec Fetherstone-Haugh followed the road ambulance from Charlton Park, racing down the M4, blue lights flashing, siren wailing, and waited till Toby arrived at Frenchay Hospital. Later, close friend of many years Alex Connors jumped into her car and drove to the hospital from her home near Bristol, and sat with Toby that terrible late afternoon, while the doctors were saving Polly's life. Dee Jordan had looked after Freddie and Jack since babies and now, with the massive upheaval to the family, she became a constant rock to them all. With Polly still in a serious condition at Frenchay over Christmas, Roger and Rachel Jowett opened up their house, and had several family members to stay. They produced a traditional Christmas day which cheered us all during that worrying time. Sixteen of us sat down to Rachel's feast and crackers, which of course included two little boys, Freddie and Jack, along with cousins Simon, Emma, Anna and Tom.

I too received many cards, phone calls, and emails during those desperately tense early weeks, as did Toby and Tory. These were a great comfort, and I thank all those family members and friends who sent them to me, and rang. There were people who had experienced similar head injuries within their families, and they rang me too. Talking to them eased the feeling of isolation, and was hugely helpful. They included car and quad bike accidents, mountain climbing, and two recent racing falls. Brother and sister-in-law Myles and Daphne Marchington offered me a bed at their house near Tetbury, whenever it was needed.

I am not sure that I have prayed too convincingly since leaving my convent boarding school many moons ago, but over those chilling weeks of uncertainty, I frequently visited the delightful little Catholic church, St. Aldhelms in Malmesbury, built in 1875, and whose open doors were a welcome sight in the dark winter evenings and, in contrast, the magnificent splendour of Salisbury cathedral, with its soaring spire and twinkling light on the top; it seemed like a hopeful star shining in the night sky.

Every Sunday for many weeks, the clergy of our local village churches of St. Oswald's, Worleston, and St. David's, Wettenhall in Cheshire, asked the congregation to pray especially for Polly, and also us, her family. A friend and neighbour, Geraldine Morgan-Wynn, requested a Mass to be said for Polly's recovery, at St. Anne's R C church in Nantwich. All these positive thoughts and vibes came from many sources and gave us strength and hope.

Polly returned home five months after her accident. She has gone on to make great strides and each year that passes brings a positive difference. The bond of her immediate family, her husband Toby and sons Freddie and Jack, her many supportive friends, and the chance to continue her career with several coaching opportunities, has given Polly significant incentive and confidence. She is able to pass on her expert knowledge and experience, and her pupils know how fortunate they are.

SIXTEEN

THE WILTON HUNT AND ASSOCIATED PONY CLUB – JACK RUSSELL TERRIERS

Children trotting on smart ponies
Rushing mothers in green wellies
sparky terriers at their heels

Jane Wallen

The wheel keeps turning and, as the years pass, ponies pop up like mushrooms as the Pony Club becomes a focus of interest once more. This time it is the Wilton Hunt branch in Wiltshire, and much of the fun I had with the Flint and Denbigh returned. Small boys are not generally known for being smitten with ponies, they require tempting or even bribing, and food often works. It was 2004 and the promise of cake and sausages had persuaded a four year old Simon to attend a meet of hounds on his squat little leading-rein pony. Eventually they discover that hunting is the best of experiences, and, of course, jumping cross-country. Boys disappear on their bikes at the mention of dressage, and as for tack cleaning, grooming and never ending mucking out – horses produce at least ten droppings every day, each one enough to fill a large bucket – this is a no-no. For this utter pony devotion and one to one care at all times, what you require, or to be blunt need – is a girl. Sure enough, in May 2003, I received another call from Christo. The perfect package had been delivered. This one was called Emma.

Many happy days have ensued following the Wilton hounds. I try to catch a glimpse of the action, running across muddy fields towed by two terriers, Sparkle and Pickle, or I wait patiently with other keen stalwarts, where the mounted field might cross a lane, using the break as an opportunity to open the bottle of wine, and grab a piece of Melton pie. I spot Tory on the smart skewbald, Pinto – another from Joe Howard – usually tucked close behind the MFH, and on her heels will be Simon on the formidable hunting cob, Bubbles, while Emma zipps along with her bouncing pony, Buttons, giving many a good horse a lead over a fence. Occasionally Christo will manage a day too. Both ponies originated from the Cheshire hunt. Good ponies find good homes, and Bubbles, who came from Phillipa Heler, is now displaying his talents with the Beaufort Pony Club, and Buttons, who came from Annabel Preece, is still with the Wilton and giving fun to the Batters twins.

When Sparkle died, along came Beetle. Sometimes I will have four tiny terrors with me. Pumpkin has joined the ranks, and Tinker loves to come, but she does tend to nip. Terriers are noisy, feisty and become uncontrollable when there is a whiff of hunting. Taking four is usually chaos and I wonder why I do it. But I cannot ignore the pricked ears when the coats and boots come out, and the questioning head on one side, 'Are we coming?'

Tinker goes and fetches her lead, and carries it trailing to the car, placing it carefully on the seat inside. If I say, 'No – not today, Tinker,' the tail droops, the ears go down, and she stares at me with a terrible wounded look. How can I resist?

'OK, you can come, Tinker, but please leave people's ankles alone.'

If you have horses, you probably have dogs, too. Driving past the line of horse boxes at a horse trial, it is very likely to be a Jack Russell that is standing guard over its patch. The original Parson Jack Russell was rough coated, mostly white, and had longish legs. With much out-crossing with other terriers, today many small dogs called Jack Russells come in all shapes, sizes and colours. Beetle is black and tan, small and sometimes fierce, with button-bright eyes. Her sister, Pumpkin, is a tan and white bundle of scruff with a pretty little face, and a coat like a mountain goat. Along with Tinker, Pumpkin belongs to Tory and family. At Christmas time Emma is likely to have her in fancy dress. It could be in an old doll's frock – probably hot pink with pants and a bonnet – or maybe a bride in frothy white tulle, and last year it was the Virgin Mary.

Polly's dog, Tag, is a sort of rescue job. She was collected at a motorway service station from Ned Pritchard – Welsh farmer, horse dealer, and once fly-weight champion boxer for Wales. Tag was lucky. Ned had planned to hand over a home-bred Jack Russell, but unfortunately a hungry sheepdog got there first. Tag – undernourished and unwanted, was found on a bleak farm in the hills of Anglesey, and presented to Polly as a last minute substitute. She grew into a much loved, bonny and happy little dog. Of all these mutts, Tinker does look like a Jack Russell. Tri-coloured with a correctly docked tail, she has become a little crusty with age. A diligent and loyal dog, while Tory rode, or lunged a horse, she spent her early adult years sitting beside a pushchair, muttering darkly and showing her teeth when on duty over her small charges. The postman is obliged to throw the post over the hedge, rather than risk a mauled trouser leg by Tinker, especially in the summertime, when he might be wearing shorts.

Beetle

Tag

Sparkle's puppies,
Pickle far left

Ned Pritchard has supplied Polly with good horses for some years. Several come over from Gorsebridge sales in Southern Ireland. Arriving on the boat from Holyhead, it is a short journey to his farm, tucked away in the vales of Anglesey. One hot summer Polly spent a day trying horses at Ned's, and I went to keep Freddie and Jack busy. After running up and down banks and through streams, and with another three horses to be scrutinised, I was running out of ideas when, lumbering free range across the farm yard came the biggest pig I have ever seen. Trotting around her were masses of piglets, bouncing in the air like mini robots. The pig then descended into a sizeable puddle, like a great pink Zeppelin, rolling, wallowing, and grunting with delectation in the cooling water, while the piglets ran around on their little trotters in the sloppy mud, wriggling their shiny snouts, and squealing with delight. Jack thought this porcine spectacle hugely entertaining, but he kept a watchful distance from the large mother pig. I was relieved at his caution, as I am sure he was thinking of joining in with the happy piglets.

As a Jack Russell owner you will recognise some, perhaps all, of the following characteristics of these little dogs. They monopolise all the best chairs in the house, and Beetle has the audacity to issue a grumble if you should wish to sit there yourself. They creep onto your knee in the car, jump up and squash themselves behind your guests at a dinner party, and although they have a cosy bed of their own, they would rather sleep on yours. They throw themselves at the door with terrible ferocity when the postman comes, and then bring you the shredded post. The fang marks ingrained on the inside of our front door would suggest we have a pet wolf, rather than a small terrier.

They like helping in the garden – especially with the digging– and they beg when you are eating, especially at dinner parties. Pickle is an expert beggar and arrives with the cheese, which is her favourite. There is – really – nothing she won't eat. She probably inherits this from her sire, as the day we took Sparkle – her mother – to be betrothed, he was in disgrace, having included in his diet the children's guinea pigs. Pickle is not the most athletic, but if she jumped onto a chair first it was easy to reach the table. She waits until there is no one around – but there was the mystery of the missing cream doughnut!

Their hunting activities are exasperating, disappearing just when you want to go out; and they stretch the nerves of those with fertile imaginations.

'Will she ever come back? Is she stuck down a hole? Has someone taken her?'

Then panic takes hold as the whole family race around the lanes and fields, searching and calling sometimes into the night, torches waving, headlights shining. Tinker is mostly white, so reasonably easy to spot, but one day Tory opened the door and took a sharp step back. Crouching outside was a very strange creature – bedraggled and brown all over. Was it a large rodent? Maybe a rare breed? Or could it be Tinker? Completely smothered in wet mud from tail to paws, it was indeed Tinker. Goodness knows where she had been.

Terriers become deaf when hunting. Pickle only comes back when she feels like it. Many is the time I have stumbled breathless over ploughed fields, ditches, through brambles, calling and searching to no avail; but then at last here she is, panting, smiling, and trundling back towards me – she is on the round side with very short legs. I am so relieved to see her, she gets a big welcome and lots of pats.

'If you are going to write a book, you will have to include sex and violence,' Geoffrey said, as I beavered away on the computer.

'Well, it's not that sort of book,' I said rather primly.

However, on reflection, I remembered an incident involving Pickle a few years ago.

'I think I might have some puppies from Pickle. Do you know a suitable dog?' I said to Sheyna Finch, a friend of mine, one day.

'What about Toast?' she said, referring to her rather handsome black and tan terrier. 'He's very experienced, he's had numerous children we know about, and probably others we don't, because he is always disappearing – "away on business," he says. You can borrow him for the day.'

So off I went to fetch Toast, and Sparkle came as chaperone, and sat on the front seat beside me. Toast was waiting in his drive, and jumped onto the back seat with Pickle, with no persuasion.

Our local town of Nantwich is a busy one, and it was market day, too, so even busier. There had been a lot of scrabbling and kerfuffle in the back as we travelled down the lanes towards Nantwich, and I pressed my foot down, keen to get through the town quickly, as through my rear view mirror I saw that Pickle and Toast had jumped off the back seat and were now up on the rear shelf, displaying their romantic antics to assorted passers-by, and we were getting some funny looks. Then, as luck would have it, the lights changed to red, and these particular lights are very long. Well, I don't know who was getting the most toasting or who the most pickling, but through my mirror, I saw the car behind me was flashing its lights and hooting, and the people inside were in fits of laughter.

But this is not the end of the story. Two days later my friend Nink Higgin rang and said, 'I've got just the right dog for your Pickle. He lives next door. Come and have some lunch, and we can put them in the greenhouse together, and watch from the kitchen window!'

So off we went again, as I thought it a good idea to make certain Pickle would have some lovely little pups. Well, after seven weeks, I said to Geoff, 'I think Pickle's a bit fatter – don't you?'

But we agreed it was difficult to tell, as Pickle does not have much of a waistline. Eventually nine weeks – the normal gestation period for dogs – stretched to ten and it became clear there would be no puppies.

'She must be a hermaphrodite,' Geoff said.

But he clearly had the wrong terminology, as there is nothing odd about Pickle – she has four legs, two ears and a tail, and certainly no extra bits. Motherhood was not for her. She was too busy keeping down the rabbits in the garden.

I have already mentioned Sparkle in this book. All tan, with one white paw and pricked ears, a brighter little dog I could never have had. She was quite simply my shadow and best friend for seventeen years, and beside me through some troubled times. In her final year, she became deaf, and a bit disorientated. Sometimes she could not find me, but I always knew where she was, because I had tied a little bell to her collar, and I could hear it tinkling as she trotted along looking for me. She was never far from my side, and out in the garden one day, she started to bark with a very insistent tone, while running first to me, and then to the hedge. 'Quiet, Sparkle,' I said rather impatiently, but she persisted, and I climbed the gate into the field; there, lying a few yards from the hedge, was a very sick calf, and I went to ring the farmer. There were always cows in that field, but Sparkle knew there was something wrong with this one.

I cannot begin to describe the heartbreak when the vet asked if I wanted to stay with her at the end. I nodded, 'Of course,' and held her in my arms as he took away her suffering, and then drove home weeping uncontrollably, with a box beside me with Sparkle inside. Geoffrey and I buried her with her collar and bell amongst the daffodils, along with the canary nearby. These are a few lines from a poem by Rudyard Kipling, which go a little way to describe how I remember Sparkle.

'I have done mostly what most men do
And pushed it out of my mind
But I can't forget if I wanted to
Four feet trotting behind.
Day after day, the whole day through
Wherever my road inclined
Four feet said "I'm coming with you"
And trotted along behind.'

Tractors and engines are usually the preference of little boys. However, Jack is different. From the age of two, he insisted on taking a copy of *Horse and Hound* to nursery rather than Thomas the Tank or Peter Rabbit. If he comes to stay I search in the shed, and find a hobby horse that neighs when you press its ear, a spotted wooden horse on wheels, pulled with a green string, and a furry black horse with white socks, standing the height of a dalmatian, which was won at the village fete. We then look in the tack room and find a hoof pick, some faded rosettes, a dandy brush, bucket and lead rope, and some pony nuts, which he enjoys mushing up with a lot of water. A garden trailer acts as a horse box and is piled high with all his horses and equipment. Jack is then happy in his own little horsey world.

The annual Easter egg hunt for the smallest members of the Pony Club was my earliest experiences with the Wilton. Held high on the downs amongst woodland and gorse, there were plenty of hiding places to fox the keenest eyes. If you happened to have a Jack Russell in your team this was an advantage. A good nose for rabbits can be transferred to chocolate eggs, especially if your name is Pickle. Eventually the appeal of the Easter egg hunt is outgrown, and we move onto Pony Club camp. Nothing has changed. A few moans about that instructor that makes us do never ending flat work, or the one that makes the jumps so *small*. But of course this annual gathering of children and ponies is always enjoyed, and there is something to be learned for all levels.

I was biding my time in the horse box, and observing a stable management session. As the only boy in his group, Simon, aged about twelve, decided some entertainment was required. The girls were ready with the Pony Club manual, but the unfortunate instructor had no chance. Simon spent the entire lesson tipping off a bucket, and lying spread-eagled on the grass, accompanied by theatrical groans. But things took on a serious turn when trying out this party piece at prep school. Before long a headed letter arrived at home.

'Simon seems to have trouble staying on his chair in class. We would advise professional tests for his fine motor skills.'

A return letter was sent forthwith.

'As Simon has no trouble at all remaining on his pony when out hunting, his fine motor skills are clearly fine!'

The Pony Club Championships have become a highlighted date in my diary once more. In 2013, after two days of hot competition, the Wilton Pony Club event team, which included Simon and his pony, Bubbles, were in a tantalisingly close second position. The final result was so tight it depended on the very last member of the leading team to complete a penalty-free cross-country round. As that vital member drew to a grinding halt at the water jump, gleeful cheers could be heard from certain members and supporters of the now victorious Wilton team. Very sporting, I must say! But whoever said, 'It's the taking part that counts, not the winning,' certainly wasn't A P McCoy.

Last year the Wilton contingent was joined by Lucy and Venetia Matthews, as Simon had been lent Venetia's horse, Charlie, and this all added to the camaraderie of the four days. No winners this time, and no disasters, and for me, being a part of it was certainly fun.

What is encouraging is the evident popularity and success of the Pony Club since it began in 1929. There is a strong competitive element, but there is nothing wrong with that. However, you only have to spend a day at a rally, or at camp, to see that all children, whatever their ability or age, are catered for, and given a chance to shine and receive a prize, whether they are sitting on a star performer or not. The emphasis is in the taking part, plus the enjoyment and companionship of ponies and horses, and in the discipline and education of how to look after them, as well as riding them.

In February this year *Horse and Hound* included an article on successful riders from non-horsey backgrounds, and listed six secrets to success. I responded to this article in a letter, which was published, and added three more to the list. First – go hunting, second – join the Pony Club, and third – find the best trainer or trainers you possibly can. Keen children like Simon and Emma have the unparalleled bonus of Tory's eventing and racing experience. Emma had a wonderful dun pony called Topic, and took the red rosette – or blue in the case of the Pony Club – so many times, that as she cantered into the jumping arena one day, someone was heard to say, 'Oh it's Emma Prior-Jowett again!'

Grace

Reggie

Myself

Simon and Emma, Pony Club

Freddie and Jack

Rome - Christopher, Barry and Lois

Christopher and Hilary Banner

Wilton Pony Club

Badminton with tractors preparing surface for 'trot up'.

Topping

Polly and Folly's last

Polly and Highland Road

Tory and Thamesdown Tootsie

Mister Tiger and Sam - yellow colours

Opening Meet - Pinto and Tory

'Are we going hunting?'

Simon and Bubbles - Pony Club Championships

Jack

Freddie

Emma and Pocket Polly

Mister Tiger and Josh Guerriero

Tiger and Sam

Wilton Pony Club - Marcus and Miranda Bird, Simon and Emma

Vicki Howell and Tiger ROR at Aintree

Geoff and Sparkle

Pony Club Championships - Roger and Rachel Jowett, Michael Tory

Katie Ayres schooling Tiger

SEVENTEEN

MISTER TIGER SHOWS HIS CLASS

After Mister Tiger's first race at Barbary Castle racecourse in early December 2011, he threw a splint; not too serious, but we had to wait another three months before he could race again. March arrived and Polly had made great strides at BIRU. With that reassurance, I was able to enjoy the point-to-point season as it unfolded, while Tiger's exploits on the race track were to engulf me in the sort of euphoria I had not experienced since the days of Tootsie, Bumble and Folly.

Tiger's next race was at Bangor-on-Dee on Sunday 11th March for the Sir Watkin William-Wynn's Point-to-Point. I was back in the fray, back at the same racecourse where I had watched Tamosaga's memorable, gutsy performance twenty-two years ago. I had been to Bangor many times in between – the racecourse is local to both North Wales and Cheshire – but this was as a spectator, oh so different when a horse you own and, in my case, have bred as well, is running. Forget a jolly day out and relaxing lunch with family and friends. My lunch comes mainly from a wine glass until the race is run, and continues after that, in either celebration or commiseration. I will be in a permanent state of inner tension, and forced equilibrium; but it is all worth it. Being in the thick of things is always my preference, and the opportunity to have a horse running is a privilege.

Despite being flat, the bank at Bangor racecourse provides good viewing, and the course is attractively situated in rural North Wales. Tiger's race – the Open Maiden – was split due to a large entry, and was the third on the card. As the previous race neared its finish, I made my way to the pre-parade paddock and waited for Tiger. I watched the other horses being saddled up, and then my horse appeared with his crossed noseband and white breastplate. Then I noticed the number on his saddle cloth – 13. Sam saw me and came over. 'How is he?' I said.

'Good,' replied Sam.

But then, keeping his options open, he added, 'It will be quite a scrum out there. I'll drop him in mid-field and then see.'

I nodded and strode towards the main parade paddock, trying to blank out Sam's words, which were annoyingly flitting about in my head.

'It will be quite a scrum out there…'

In the paddock, Geoffrey joined me, along with Sam's parents – Robert and Rachel. There were plenty of spectators leaning on the rails as the horses paraded. Tiger had matured in his physique in the three months since his last race. He is not a big horse – just 16.1hh on his tiptoes. His head, which is very dark bay, has a prominent white star, and is slightly dished (concave) harking back to his Arabian ancestors. His forehead is broad, and his eyes wide set. His expression is inquisitive and alert. He has a correctly proportioned, athletic frame and a well-sprung rib cage, denoting heart room, with a good slope to his shoulder, giving him an easy swinging step. He looked a class horse, and I felt a sense of pride watching him. I spotted Roy and Mary Kinsey in the crowd and waved. Tiger had spent many months as a two and three year old munching their acres of grass, when mine had run out.

Time ticked by and out came the jockeys. It is not difficult to spot Sam. Twelve stone is the compulsory weight carried by all horses in point-to-points, unless the horse is a four year old, a mare, or ridden in a ladies' race. At six foot three inches, Sam tops the other jockeys and is as lean as a lathe. Perhaps I exaggerate, but his saddle is paper thin, and about the size of the one on a rocking horse. The bell rang, the jockeys were quickly legged up, and horses began to leave the paddock; Tiger chomped on his bit, jogging impatiently, his neck tight and tensing now, wanting to be released. Running alongside him, Robert swung Sam into the plate, and they cantered off.

I had watched Tory winning races, and Polly winning gold medals, pulses pumping as they both set sail for the challenge of jumping huge fences and galloping flat out across the countryside. I had been part of that family team of horse and rider, and was as proud as punch, as was Christopher, of our daughters; but the success was first and foremost theirs. This felt different. I had bred Tiger and watched him entranced as he darted across the field as a foal, twirling, prancing and free as air, and then grow into a well-put-together three year old – he never went through a plain stage as many young horses do – and finally develop into a good-looking, smart racehorse. There is something rather satisfying about saying you own a racehorse, whatever level it might be – it is, after all, the 'Sport of Kings'.

I was on a knife edge of excitement and nerves. Nothing from Tiger's first race had given me especially high expectations, but I knew I would be disappointed if he ran a bad race, or was pulled up, or the worst, lay sprawled on the ground. His was a large field of fifteen runners, and a good run, perhaps finishing in the first four, would be encouraging, and hold promise for next time. I headed off down the hill towards the course, and walked quickly past the last fence on the final circuit. Unable to stand still, I paced between the first two fences, and gazed into the distance as the horses jostled at the start. The flag went down, and now I stood rigid, scanning the surge of colour coming towards me, looking hard for Sam's green, black and yellow colours.

The going was good, and horses came thundering across the turf in an ever-increasing crescendo, the noise pounding in my ears as they came closer and closer. Noticing Tiger bunched between five others, I felt myself tense as he rose to jump. I heard the whoosh and thwack as the combined power of muscled horse flesh and crouching jockeys cleared the brush. Tiger landed safely, and the cavalcade disappeared into the country – just streamlined specks now, moving rhythmically along the white rails in the distance. Impossible to see what is happening out there, but at last they come back into view. The race is three miles, covering two and a quarter circuits of the track, and the bends at Bangor are tight. Sam has Tiger nicely placed in fourth, letting him bowl along and in touch. As they come towards me with another circuit to go, I see the white star standing out like a beacon on his dark bay face – so far, so good, and my heart lifts as the commentator gives a reassuring, 'Mister Tiger is travelling well,' as they pass the judge.

Into the second circuit, and the field has split, the first six going on convincingly, led by the grey Courageous Dove, and Tiger staying on comfortably in fourth. With five left to jump, my excitement has moved into overdrive. I noticed Sam, bent low but still, was tight on the heels of the three in front of him, and there was no doubting his attitude – it was competitive. The horses swung right-handed approaching the fourth from last, and I stretched up on my toes, leaning forward and gripping the rails, trying to spot Sam on the far side of the leaders. Had he caught them up? Then I heard the commentator.

'With four left to jump Head Over Heels has taken up the lead, but it is Mister Tiger who just pokes his nose in front as they land together. The gap is widening between a leading group of three, and the rest of the field, and Courageous Dove has now come up to dispute the lead with Mister Tiger.'

Now I can see them clearly as they gallop towards me once again, and my heart is racing – racing – racing. My horse is leading the field, and pulling away. The commentator continues, his voice quickening as they jump the penultimate.

'Mister Tiger and Sam Allwood, in the yellow colours, land a long way clear and head towards the final fence. Head Over Heels is challenging, but Mister Tiger jumps an easy length clear, and accelerates on the run in. This is going to be one for Sam Allwood as Mister Tiger gallops on well to win.'

How can I give a true description and eloquence to the emotions that overwhelmed me as I realised my horse was going to win, and then watched him sweep past the post ahead of the field? I cannot – without sounding ridiculous. But that is how it is with horses. They reach to the core of your being and your soul. There is something about them, something heroic, that carries you high above the clouds, soaring like an eagle. This is no exaggeration. Just watch the ecstatic faces of winning connections at the Cheltenham Festival, or any race meeting.

This was a first win for Tiger, and like that very first win for us at Tweseldown, it was far from my expectations. It is a different sensation to setting off as favourite, and feeling that you should win – that is pressure, however good it feels when it happens. Thinking back, there was a quiet confidence about Sam before the race, although I was too preoccupied to pick it up at the time. But good jockeys and trainers study the form of the opposition, and know how their horses are as they watch and ride them in training. Tiger was beginning to show true ability. There was just one sticky moment in that race. The horse, still at times green, had skewed over the last fence as he hung left towards the paddock, and Sam, aware of the second horse getting closer, gave him a couple of reminders on the run in. Sam knew he had it in the bag but was taking no chances. Tiger responded, remembered what he was there for, and sprinted away, winning by six lengths, with more to give.

That marvellous day was manna from heaven, justification for the many weeks of patient waiting, and a great weight lifted. My horse had proved he could win, and in good company. The glowing feeling of satisfaction smoulders on within, and brings a quiet smile forever, but the high is like a burst of golden bubbles from the best champagne, and lasts a relatively short time. It is no wonder you want to have the whole experience again and again. The success provided a salve to ease the twitches and tensions, as I mentally ticked off the days until the next time.

The North Staffordshire point-to-point is situated on the Sandon estate, about four miles from Stone in Staffordshire. It is held on the Saturday of Easter weekend, and is a well-supported and popular day. Tiger was entered for the combined North Staffs, and the Meynell and South Staffs Hunt Members race, which is open to all levels and was first on the card. Despite two higher-rated Open horses entered, Tiger was 6/4 on and tipped as favourite by the bookies, but anything can happen, and often does, in a race.

The pressure of expectation kept chipping at my thoughts, but I was excited and looking forward to the day, as Tory was coming up to watch with Christo, Simon and Emma. It is a long way from Salisbury to Staffordshire, and it mattered a lot to me that Tiger showed his best to my family. Our good friends Tony and Frances Wedd were joining us; Tony was later to generously chip in on a share with Tiger, so all in all I wanted everyone to enjoy themselves. Geoff had stocked the car with large glasses, and plenty of alcoholic celebrations and comforts – hopefully it would be the former. Tony also likes a punt, and a win would put the extra gloss on the day for him.

The course at Sandon is attractively set below the car parks, trade stands, and paddock, so viewing is excellent, apart from one small part hidden by trees. This time Tiger knew what it was all about. The flag went down, he set his neck, eyes popping, and grabbed the bit, wanting to fly. Sam, however, had other ideas, and made him wait; three miles is a test of stamina as well as speed, and top rated The King of Angels was a seasoned campaigner and proven stayer. Sam tucked Tiger in behind the first three, and the reins remained taut for several fences, as the horse thought he knew better. But once into the second circuit, he settled well and, looming up on the outside of the leaders, Sam gave the rein and allowed him to overtake. This he did – like a knife through a slab of butter. Only The King of Angels stayed with him, and he was now three lengths back. But there were still four fences, and a distance to travel.

I stood alone watching, heart thumping with every stride, and although Tiger was travelling the better, there was no doubting the resolve of the second jockey, who was tracking Sam with determination, and a niggling thought entered my head.

The King of Angels is a proven stayer.

With just three fences left, the crowds of watching spectators had become noticeably vocal, and the commentary was getting louder.

'Mister Tiger is stretching on ahead and takes a *beautiful* jump at the seventeenth. They gallop on to the penultimate, but The King of Angels hasn't finished yet, and is now on his tail. Sam Allwood takes a quick look behind; Mister Tiger lengthens his stride, and pulls away as they accelerate towards the finish.'

There were whoops and shouts all around me as Tiger won easily in the end. I was thrilled and relieved, and it felt rather strange that all sorts of people that I didn't even know, but who must have backed Tiger, were jumping up and down, and shouting and roaring for my horse as he sprinted through the finish; and I felt like shouting too, 'That's *my* horse, that's *my* horse.'

I ran down the hill to greet them, determined to lead Tiger in. Sam leant down and patted him on the neck, and I had a job keeping up, as Tiger, still full of running, pulled his way towards the winner's enclosure, while I puffed along beside him, smiling broadly. It was becoming clear that stamina was running through his veins, just like his dam, Thamesdown Tootsie. We were presented with champagne and an enormous silver cup, engraved with a well-known name in racing circles, The Bill Tellwright Memorial Trophy.

Tabley Hall in Cheshire was the seat of the Leicester family. The Palladian mansion, set in extensive parkland with its shimmering expanse of lake, is in the north of the county near Knutsford, and that is where we travelled on Sunday 20th May to watch Mister Tiger once again. By now he was making a name for himself, and was listed as the leading novice horse in the area. He had also moved up a grade and would face tougher opposition. Expectations were mounting. The meeting attracts plenty of runners, and with the city of Manchester within commuting distance, there are large crowds, and it is well-sponsored. Amongst the sponsors, with a marquee providing a sumptuous champagne lunch, expertly organised by step-daughter Stella Heap, and situated on the run in to the final fence, is the Manchester Tennis and Racquets Club. The club dates back to 1876, and the tennis – played on an indoor court – is that of Real Tennis which was played in Tudor times by Henry VIII at Hampton Court Palace. The luncheon club, with its leather armchairs, large white-clothed dining tables, and traditional food, is patronised by many of the great and the good of Manchester's business world, and the county of Cheshire.

The marquee was packed with members and guests and, as a member of the club, Geoffrey had a large table booked, and several friends were gathered. I knew most of the people in that tent had put money on Tiger. The pressure of expectation or, the higher you fly, the harder you can fall. As the time for the first race became imminent, the Cheshire Forest hounds, in good cry, and following a scarlet-coated huntsman blowing his horn, flashed past the sponsored marquees. This colourful show heralded the start of the racing entertainment. The thrills, and probably some spills, were about to commence.

Tiger's race was fourth on the card, and a good field of runners collected in the paddock, overlooked by the imposing square facade of Tabley Hall. I made my way to the paddock well in time and, out of curiosity, pushed through the crowds amassed by the bookies to look at the odds on the boards. I was fairly sure that Tiger would be posted as the favourite, but I wondered whether there was anything else fancied too. And then my eyes gaped. Flashing across the top of the boards was Tiger's name in neon lights. You couldn't miss them.

'All bets except Mister Tiger,' they shouted in lit-up colour.

Tiger was such a hot favourite, so certain to win, that the bookies were taking no more bets on him. I should have been more nervous than ever, but I wasn't – I felt a rush of adrenalin. It was thrilling to see his name up there, so prominent and full of expectation.

Entering the paddock, I felt pumped up and rather bullish, almost on a high before anything had happened. This was foolish; horse racing is a risk sport for both horse and jockey. But I sensed nothing would touch Mister Tiger – provided he remained upright.

Joining Robert and Rachel, Geoffrey, and several other owners and trainers, we engaged in some light banter, filling in the last few minutes. Then Sam emerged with the other jockeys, and touched his cap to me as owner in the traditional way. We had a little chat, the bell rang, Sam was legged up on an already eager Tiger, and off they cantered to the start, escorted by two members of the hunt. A couple of horses plunged keenly, while Tiger set his head, ears pricked. He was focused – not a green novice any more. He knew what was expected of him – would he deliver?

It was a fresh, sunny day and I set off to the middle of the course on my own. Crowds milled round and out of the corner of my eye I noticed the horse ambulance with the large green cross parked near the track, but I hurried on, keeping my imagination under orders – there is always that lurking fear. I stood under the canopy of a leafy chestnut tree, and waited. From there I could see most of the course.

Apart from one wet patch down by the lake, the going was good, and the horses set off at a strong pace, with the orange and brown colours of John Wilson's Gunner BB taking up the lead. Sam settled Tiger midfield in fifth place, and they swung along comfortably for the first circuit. With another complete circuit to go, I noticed the first five were bunched together. These pulled away from the rest, and Sam tracked the leaders on the outside. Passing the judge, a horse fell, rolled over, got up and kept galloping. I let out a sigh of relief as Tiger was not impeded.

A fast moving group of mostly bays and a couple of greys stretched on towards the lake – powerful, electrifying. Sheep, unconcerned, cropped the grass in the fields beyond. With fourteen fences jumped, the horses approached the sixth from home. Shielding my eyes, I felt a thump of confidence, as I spotted the unmistakably balanced outline of Sam, and the dark bay shape of Tiger, going well. But the pace was increasing, and now Sam put the pressure on his horse. Tiger responded, and moved up a gear fast. The fence loomed, and Sam saw a brilliant stride from a long way off. Tiger winged the brush, gaining ground, and landed with the leaders. Three left to jump, and the pace sharpened up again, jockeys crouched lower, and a couple of horses got reminders. Several had dropped back, noticeably tired, but Tiger was keen, sharp, and on the bridle.

Now, as the horses swung round the right-hand bend, and into the straight towards home, my eyes gaped for the second time that day. I saw Sam's yellow colours ablaze and streaking ahead, while Tiger was hurtling across the turf like a fresh horse. He was ten lengths – fifteen lengths – in front of the pack, and gathering speed all the time. As he swept past the yelling marquees I ran towards the finishing post; I knew, that nothing could touch my horse; he only had to jump the last fence.

I was stepping back seventeen years. Tiger was emulating Tootsie, his dam, and he stormed through the finish, an easy fourteen lengths clear of the second horse, while the rest trailed in behind. Sam stood up in his stirrups in triumph, and we made our way to the winner's enclosure yet again.

Winning in front of a home crowd just adds that extra bit of chutzpah, and the MTRC marquee was lit up with cheers and popping corks. Tiger had looked imperious, and beaten several decent horses with impressive ease. It was a very good feeling indeed.

At the end of 2012 season Tiger had picked up several accolades. He was listed as one of the leading six year old horses in the country, and one of the most prolific winners. Sam finished the season tying for the Area Senior Gentlemen's Championship.

Our house was stuffed with silver that year. I had watched Tory and Polly many times receiving prizes, but it was quite a novel experience for me, and judging from the informed opinions and write-ups about Tiger, I had a very good horse indeed for next season. I knew Sam was keen to do a Hunter Chase, and to qualify Tiger for the Red Mills sponsored race which is held at Cheltenham racecourse.

The following year I went to watch him on his final gallop before his first race. It was a bitterly cold day as, muffled up with other owners, we gathered together while six horses trotted up the all-weather track in pairs, and then galloped three times down the five and a half furlongs. On the third stretch I watched with eyes wide. Tiger was still straining on the bridle, flicking out his toes, and fighting to get in front – it was clear he was fit, and ready to go racing again, and I couldn't wait to see him.

Horse racing is not just a risk sport physically. Emotionally, mentally everyone involved will be on a permanent roller-coaster, liable to plunge any time. I would love to tell you of more wonders from Mister Tiger, but it seems I had had my 5 percent. I was going to have to bear up and endure the other 95.

Two days after that gallop, Sam rang and the bottom fell out of my dreams. Tiger had strained a tendon. It is just about the worst news to hear. A 'leg', whether mild or serious, means a minimum of twelve months out of action. I had made the mistake of bringing horses back too quickly before. Tiger was a young horse and a good one. I decided to give him fifteen months. He was given stem-cell treatment but, in hindsight, I would not do this again, as I am not sure the treatment is sufficiently proven to be successful.

We did try Tiger again, and his first race on his return, with accomplished jockey Josh Guerrerio in the plate this time, was encouraging. But not long after that he had a fall at Bangor. Sam rang the next day with the gutting news that he was injured again, and in some pain. I replaced the phone, and put my head in my hands in despair and desolation. Later that day I drove slowly to Sam's yard with a bag of carrots for Tiger, and a heart like a lump of granite in my stomach.

I contacted the Retraining of Racehorses scheme – ROR – which is under the umbrella of the British Horseracing Authority, and started to make plans for a new career. Tiger would need several more months recovering, and Sam brought him home to me. We sadly swapped head collars and rugs, and I watched the empty box drive out of the gate. Tiger was then treated by Campbell Thompson at Nantwich equine vets. He was sedated and given platelet-rich plasma by centrifugation. Blood was taken from his neck and injected into the site of injury. He stood quietly, which was vital, as injecting into exactly the right spot was crucial.

Tiger is a beautiful light mover and a good jumper. He has spent several months with eventer Katie Ayres and jockey Rob Jarrett, and Katie completed four BE events with him successfully. Katie then had a bad fall on another horse at Chatsworth. Tiger is now back with Sam, while partner and top assistant Vicki Howell has taken him to the prestigious ROR show held in the spectacular indoor school at Aintree racecourse. This was a fascinating day out as we observed many beautiful ex-racehorses. The champion that day was a horse by Galileo which had originally come from Jonjo O'Neill. I was also able to admire the superb statue of Red Rum which holds pride of place at Aintree.

What will Tiger's next chapter be? Perhaps that will be another story.

EIGHTEEN

REFLECTIONS – SPONSORSHIP – EVENTING MOTHERS

I do not ask to see the distant scene – one step enough for me.

Taken from Lead Kindly Light
by Cardinal John Henry Newman.

Light is only given to us gradually bit by bit, but we are always given enough to see what we have to do next, and that when we have taken that step, which has been lit for us, we shall see the next step, but only the next, illuminated. To attempt to see several steps ahead, or the end of the path, is not only futile but also self-defeating.

In 2014, about two years after Polly's accident, she took part in the Bath Half Marathon in aid of BIRU. With her was a former patient who had sustained a rugby head injury, Polly's trainer, Ollie, who helped her with fitness, and a few supporters to cheer them along. Polly's consultant, Angus Graham, had told me that her recovery would continue for up to five years, and perhaps beyond, but that the rate would slow down with each passing year. The Bath Half is over thirteen miles, and at that time Polly's mobility and balance were shaky – she could barely run, and was helped by long walking poles. Ollie, carrying a watch, a donation bucket, and sometimes the poles, ran alongside her, telling her when to walk, and when to run. Anyone who has watched or taken part in marathons has seen the thousands who start, and the many that drop off. It was a Sunday, and wondering how things were going, I keyed in Bath Marathon on the computer, scrolled down, clicked BIRU competitors, and there they were on the screen, this little band of troopers, coming in almost last, but triumphantly amongst cheers. Just visible, running along the final yards with them, was a small boy; I recognised Freddie, and on the other side of the barriers, striding along, was Toby, with Jack on his shoulders.

During her eventing career, Polly had the benefit of the best trainers in the sport, some of whom I have already mentioned, but add to these Dot Willis, and Senior team coach, Yogi Breisner. Polly has given radio and newspaper interviews, and she is currently booked for a thirty minute talk in aid of Headway, the brain injury charity.

There are sometimes grumbles about the NHS, but when it comes to critical and life-threatening care, our family's experience of the dedication and expertise of the medical team at Frenchay Hospital, and later at BIRU, was exceptional. Included in this tribute are the paramedics and air ambulance doctors who gave vital on-site treatment to Polly.

Since writing this book, Frenchay Hospital has been demolished, and a brand new hospital has been built in Bristol.

Acquiring sponsorship in eventing is not easy. The sport does not lie particularly well with non-equestrian companies, as media coverage is limited. Finance at the top of the sport is a big issue. Without financial backing, and you need gargantuan amounts to maintain a large stable of good horses, it is difficult to survive. Buying and selling horses, and teaching, is the bread and butter, but it is the owners and sponsors who will enable you to remain at the top, and unless you or your parents are very wealthy, the house will have to be sold! This, of course, is extreme, but it has been known. An Arab prince in the support team would be splendid, but they are usually seen in the manicured paddocks of flat racing at Ascot or The Derby.

If your family are well-known, or they have had previous success in the equine world, then this advantage can open doors regarding owners and sponsorship, but results must still be produced. The participation and success of Zara Phillips is undoubtedly a boost to the publicity and image of eventing. Zara's inclusion in the World Equestrian Games 2014, soon after the birth of her daughter, was a possible gamble that paid off, and demonstrated how first-rate she is under pressure. Her inclusion immediately ignited media interest, with a front page picture of her in The Daily Telegraph.

From our experience, the best way to acquire sponsorship is through personal contacts, your friends, their friends, a chance meeting, social or business. We produced a glossy brochure and wrote to many high-profile companies, but the results were disappointing. Polly did some cold calling locally, and succeeded with Ifor Williams Trailers. Her main sponsors, Samuel Banner & Co., TNT International, T. Norbury & Co. and Holland and Holland, came through friends and contacts. Cultivate your knowledge, your charm and appear efficient. Everything helps.

Caroline Pratt had her base in Cheshire. She educated several horses for me in the latter years, and no one produced a young horse better. Caroline had some loyal owners, but finance was a permanent headache for her. She was very down when the lottery funding she had been allocated was cut off. I went to Burghley not long after, and Caroline stood under the trees by the dressage arenas with her horse Imperial Cavalier. It was a blazing hot day but, thin as a rake, Caroline was trembling like a leaf. The next day she was killed from a fall on the cross-country at the water fence. Pressure of the wrong kind can be a dangerous thing.

During the 2012 Olympics in London, Charlotte Dujardin, from another equestrian discipline – Grand Prix Dressage – made a significant impact on the 'non-horsey' public. The television coverage of this event became known as the 'dancing horses', and attracted a huge audience. Charlotte's performance in the freestyle dressage to music, I found bewitching. The choreography of music chosen was masterful. It included Elgar's *Land of hope and glory*, Parry's *I vow to thee my country*, and the chimes of Big Ben. So imaginative and fitting for the occasion, and superbly interpreted by Charlotte and Valegro. The pair repeated the success at the World Equestrian Games 2014, and once again I noticed the harmony Charlotte has with her horse, with a marked fluidity compared with some of the other European riders, who resembled mechanical puppets. However, I am no expert when it comes to Grand Prix Dressage. I just know a rigid rider, and a tight-mouthed horse, is not attractive to watch. I rather like the Spanish horses with their sense of theatre.

Mary King must be the epitome of someone who started with neither substantial finance nor an equestrian background, and yet she has managed to balance her career at the very top, together with marriage and children, successfully – a remarkable achievement. How has she done it? There were the obvious assets; talent, dedication, loyal owners, etc. But I recall many years ago, while still trailing behind Polly at events, seeing a lady pushing a baby buggy, bumping over the uneven terrain, and keeping up with someone high on a horse on the way to the dressage arena. Perhaps she had some fly spray for the horse and a grooming brush tucked away in the buggy, too. That someone was Mary King, and the lady nobly pushing the buggy was Mary's mother, with granddaughter Emily. Mary herself pays tribute to her mother in her autobiography, and this maternal dedication would continue for years to come, including a second child. Mary stood proudly on the podium many times, but in my mind – as if quietly standing behind her – I can see that person who gamely pushed the baby buggy. Interestingly, that baby is now riding for the British Young Rider squad.

In those days, it was team Ginny Holgate – later Leng – which dominated the sport. Parked next to the Holgate box, I noticed a horse dive down to grab some grass. It was immediately hauled up with a certain force, accompanied by a vocal boom that resonated across the park, 'YOU ARE HERE TO DO A JOB NOT TO EAT *GRAASS*'.

It came, of course, from the imposing figure of senior management and resident trainer – Dot Willis. Ginny was dedicated and talented, but it was not difficult to see who held the conductor's baton – Ginny's mother, Heather Holgate, tall, imperious, svelte, hair coiffed, with, on that summer's day, close-fitted white shorts, from which emerged tanned legs. Here were female cogs in the wheel of success. On occasions at the major Internationals, the late Pat Manning – Fellow of the British Horse Society – was drafted in to instil that extra bit of 'win' power. This relentless commitment was what made team Holgate so powerful at that time. This was horse and rider training at its most professional.

Elaine Straker was another formidable eventing mother of that era. She had an eye for finding horses for daughter Karen, with class and talent. The thoroughbred Get Smart must be one of the outstanding event horses of all time. He completed Badminton six times consecutively, apart from a one year break. To those that follow racing, this could be compared to a horse completing the Grand National six times in a row, with just one break.

Lady Doreen Prior-Palmer was rather different, though I expect equally influential in the background. I first met her when she was a member of the Young Rider selection panel, the year Polly rode for the team, at Rotherfield Park in 1990. It was some years after, that I was walking the cross-country course at Punchestown in Ireland, when I became aware of someone sort of hiding beside a tree. It was Lucinda Green's mother, and Lucinda was, of course, at that moment galloping round the course. It was well past her glory days, but as Lady Prior-Palmer and I acknowledged each other, she smiled ruefully, and said, 'Watching doesn't get any easier.'

With regard to the parents of other sports stars, Seb Coe said that his trainer father, Peter, could be brutal at times, but their very close relationship was the lynchpin to Seb's great success. Andy Murray's mother, Judy, is a constant presence, and has taken some criticism, but it was she who first put a tennis racquet in his hand. Olympic gold medallist, Victoria Pendleton, has said that her keen cycling father pushed her remorselessly in her early career, but acknowledges his significant influence on her success. She defied all sceptics in her brilliant ride in the Cheltenham Foxhunters, after just a year of riding horses, and proved that talent and discipline in one sphere can be repeated in another.

There is a fine line between positive encouragement and over pushing, and it is difficult to accomplish that line. However, I well recall someone saying to me, 'You cannot push a child who does not want to be pushed – they will feign illness or find a way to avoid taking up the task. A keen person will push themselves, irrespective of anyone else.' I would say that the greatest lesson to be learnt, whatever the end view, is perseverance and, with horses, infinite patience. I wish I had had more patience, but that comes with experience. Andrew Nicholson's win at Badminton 2017 after something like thirty-five attempts is an excellent example of perseverance.

No rider at the top of his or her game can manage without an expert team at the practical level, but from observation it is the girls who rely more on the psychological back-up. Confidence and belief are crucial, and this can inspire a horse to go the extra mile, too. Boys seem to have this element of 'gung ho' more naturally than girls. Surveys have found this at schools, to the point where some schools include, in their curriculum for girl pupils, how to be assertive and push through doubts and disappointment.

The fact that there are still riders competing at the top, in their middle forties, is a positive thing. Amongst these are William Fox-Pitt, Pippa Funnell and Tina Cook. These three riders were all in gold medal winning teams with Polly over twenty-five years ago. An amazing statistic and all credit to the three of them. Many years ago, I noticed a young girl showjump at Aldon Horse Trials; she was probably about sixteen. I had sat near the arena for ages, watching, and no one had caught my eye, but this girl did; her name was Tina Gifford. One of William's owners is the delightfully outspoken lady from the north, Cath Witt. Cath lives less than a mile from us here in Cheshire. She is a great supporter of the sport, and I was so pleased when her horse Park Lane Hawk, ridden by William, took the trophy at Burghley in 2011.

From the younger ranks Oliver Townend showed early promise as a Junior back in 1998. I had been asked to join the selection panel for the Junior European team, and we had gathered at Windsor for the National Championships. I gave Oliver the prize for the best turned out horse on the final day. Most of the horses had been plaited up by grooms or mummys, but Oliver, at fifteen years of age, and possibly the only boy, had plaited his own horse.

I was looking forward to being a part of the scene again, now from the other side of the fence. Having been through the whole caboodle of selection trials several times over, I found it intriguing observing the torment of twenty-five sets of parents watching their future Olympians endure the rigours of five days of scrutiny for the privilege of wearing a Union Jack on their jacket. Had I been like that, I wondered. Is it worth it? Is it really so important? Having a go takes spirit, and life without challenges would be a waste. Finding a balance is the hard bit, but in the greater scheme of things absolutely essential. The boulders get larger as you climb higher. It is only in hindsight you see the bigger picture. It can be heady stuff when your offspring is picked out by a selection panel. You have to set your own boundaries then stick by them.

The price of some top International ponies and Junior horses is mind-boggling. You could buy a nice house in Surrey, or even a detached in Wilmslow, complete with decorated, wrought iron security gates. For those unfamiliar with this part of Cheshire, the expensive town of Wilmslow, south of Manchester, is often known as 'footballers wives'.

Undiluted success is not necessarily good for young people – life is just not like that – and very expensive animals can flatter inexperienced riders. Our best horses and ponies were rarely the most expensive. It takes years of success and failure to become expert in any sphere.

Two other Juniors, at the time I was a selector, were Harry Mead and Kitty King. Like Oliver Townend, they stood out amongst the many hopefuls that came forward. The chairman of the Junior selectors when I first joined the panel was Viscount Michael Allenby. It was under his leadership that the Junior team won a gold medal in Poland in 1998. I found Michael an approachable and kind person. I was interested to read, in his obituary in *The Telegraph*, about his concern for the welfare of animals, particularly horses, and his valuable chairmanship of the International League for the Protection of Horses.

No horse wants to fall, either in eventing or racing. There are some – the quicker thinkers – who will find a fifth leg and remain upright, and there are others who, when asked the extra question, will take an opportunity to say 'No – can't do it.' There has been a huge leaning towards warmbloods in eventing, because of their ability to shine in the dressage. The breed has fined down over the years, and since the less stamina-testing short format was brought in, a touch maybe an advantage. To clarify the term warmblood, these horses come between a thoroughbred, which is fiery, fleet of foot and mind, and hot-blooded, and a heavier type, which is cold-blooded, and which were bred as work horses and war horses, either to pull or carry weight. Warmbloods originated on the continent in Germany, Sweden or Holland. Thoroughbreds were bred to race, and this is reflected in their paces and in their temperament. The movement of thoroughbreds is flatter and nearer to the ground, making them faster but giving them less cadence. The warmblood lacks the speed but has power, which is an advantage in dressage and in show jumping.

At its best, I believe the thoroughbred is the superior, but only if his sometimes mettlesome and sensitive nature is developed in a positive partnership with the rider. The one outstanding quality he has is his stamina, and this harks back to his Arabian ancestry, when these small horses were required to carry the nomadic Arabs across miles of sun-baked deserts for long days, and with little water. Irish or pony blood – perhaps an eighth or a sixteenth – can be a plus in a thoroughbred. Successful competition horses which have the resilience to remain completely sound in wind, heart, legs and feet, is essential, but also rare, as greater stress is put on them as they move up the grades. Learning how to manage a horse with any soundness issue, in conjunction with a trusted equine vet and farrier, is vital when competing at the top of equestrian sport.

Britain's result at the European Championships 2015 was a silver medal, but there was an enormous gap between Germany – gold, and Britain – silver. The Colonels would not be pleased! Who might fill that gap in Rio? It could be the Aussies and Kiwis – ineligible at the European Championships – who will be stepping up the heat. Germany's Michael Jung is today's eventing phenomenon. His ride round the cross-country at Blair Castle, on the eight year old Fisher Takinou, was a demonstration of supreme artistry.

Both the sport of National Hunt racing, and eventing at the top level, can present tough demands physically. Injuries will happen, some serious. I believe it is important to have another string to your bow, and to do your best at that, too. Confidence breeds success, and can be a spring-board to other things. British International Harry Mead, who went to university, culminating in a degree, wrote an interesting article in *Horse and Hound* on this topic earlier this year. On a rather lighter note, when Sam Allwood's schoolteacher suggested to his parents that it would be a good idea if he read more, his mother said. 'Well, he reads *The Racing Post* every day!'

The names of horses are interesting. Owners give their horses names for many different reasons. Some are named after places, or famous people, or maybe animals. There have been horses on the eventing circuit called Overdraft and In the Red, or other similar connotations with the sport. Usually these present no problem to the officials, except

I do recall a horse one year called Buck Off. This is quite appropriate in many ways. However, Buck Off can sound rather different when called repeatedly over a cross-country tannoy. The owner, who was a bit of a wag, was told to choose another name.

I have relived many memories, some misty with the passing of time. I can still marvel at Tootsie, now aged thirty-two, hightailing away when Peter Handley the farrier comes to trim, and I can stroke Tiger's nose, and watch him with interest. Perhaps I will have that thrill – that incomparable thrill – of seeing him gallop and jump once more.

I will always turn my head to look at a horse, or even a humble donkey. From a herd of wild ponies, cropping the heath on Exmoor, to fine thoroughbreds galloping like the wind across the turf of England. Mighty Shire horses, fiery Arabians with their ancient heritage. In the animal kingdom, they are all God's masterpieces, given to us to share their gifts of speed, power and freedom. Every year I watch the Trooping of the Colour. We are the envy of the world for our pageantry, and seeing those splendid horses and riders – plumed and proud as they make their way down The Mall, led by the magnificent coloured Drum horses – is a sight to behold.

Sometimes, when I am writing this book late into the night, alone except for the moon and stars, or equally, on a beautiful spring day, fresh and green with the sun shining, I have a sensation that those horses and ponies who gave me so much fun, pride, tears and elation are nearby. I have not mentioned them all, but I remember them all.

One Christmas, at the age of about four, Freddie was asked what he received from Father Christmas. He thought about it, and then said, 'Ladders and Snakes.' How very true to life was his interpretation of the title of the game. Having climbed a few ladders, the snakes will always be around to slither down. The good thing is that, however many snakes there are, if you keep throwing the dice, you will eventually climb enough ladders to reach the top of the board, and then perhaps start all over again.

Last year I went to Badminton, but not to watch the stars. I was watching a twelve year old Emma take part in the Mitsubishi Motors Cup, which is a competition that takes place the day before the big event, on a separate course around the splendid park, and within sight of the Great House. It is one of the latest innovative ideas for amateur and up and coming young riders. Excitement was at fever pitch. Was I expected to keep a lid on the proceedings – I don't think so.

Once again I paced the ground from fence to fence, towed along by two terriers. But they were not pulling in the same direction. You might have seen me; one small dog is black and tan, and the other, a little round, is all tan. She tugged me with great single-mindedness towards the fast food area and the burger bar. Her name, as you have guessed, is Pickle!

Pickle

POSTSCRIPT

Since completing this book, The British team has won Gold at the 2017 European Championships.

Thamesdown Tootsie died in her paddock in October 2017, aged thirty-two years. She is very much missed.

References

James, Jeremy. *The Byerley Turk,* Merlin Unwin Books, Ludlow (2007)

Pinfold, John. *Hoylake Race Course and the Beginnings of the Royal Liverpool Golf Club.*

Ian & Marilyn Boumphrey Prenton Wirral (2002)

Horse and Hound (1984) (1989) (1990)

O'Neil, Jim. *Hoylake History*

Sparkle

ACKNOWLEDGEMENTS

I would like to acknowledge Mike Tucker's generous response to my request for a few words for the cover of this book. They were written just four weeks before his untimely death in March 2018. Mike's contribution to the equestrian world was without equal. Equestrian commentator for the BBC for 40 years, Mike covered six Olympic Games including London and Rio.

I would like to thank my friends Andrew Hamilton and Dr. Lesley Randles for their excellent critique, to Carol Stoddart and Jan Heys, who read the chapters on Polly's accident, and to John Ingram who perused the illustrations. All gave me much encouragement and helpful comments.

I would like to express my appreciation for the support I received in my equine pursuits, from Christopher in the early days, and Geoffrey in later years.

Last but not least to Tory and Polly for their brilliant and brave riding.

Red deer, Isle of Rum